THE
HIDDEN WAY

THE HIDDEN WAY

by

C. Cyril Eastwood
BD, PhD, FRHistS

My Guide and I upon that hidden way
entered, returning to the world of light...

Dante's Divine Comedy

BRECHINSET PUBLICATIONS

BRECHINSET PUBLICATIONS
7-11 King Street, Ipswich, Suffolk, England IP1 1EG

ISBN 0—9507064—5—0

Designed and typeset by Brechinset, Ipswich, Suffolk
Illustrations by Oona Harte
Printed and bound by Robert Hartnoll Ltd., Bodmin, Cornwall

Contents

To
Simon, Sarah and Ben

Acknowledgements

The author is grateful to the following for permission to use material from their publications:

Anthony Sheil Associates Ltd., for material from *Contemplating Now* by Monica Furlong, (Hodder), © Monica Furlong 1971.

Collins Publishers for material from *Memories, Dreams and Reflections* by C. G. Jung, 1967; *Silent Music* by W. Johnston, 1974.

Constable & Co. Ltd., for material from H. J. Blackham's Introduction in *Objections to Humanism*, 1963. Published in Pelican Books 1965.

David Higham Associates Ltd., for lines from 'Light breaks where no sun shines' from *Collected Poems* by Dylan Thomas, published by J. M. Dent.

Faber and Faber Ltd., Reprinted by permission of Faber and Faber Ltd., and Harcourt Brace Jovanovich Inc., New York, from *Four Quartets* by T. S. Eliot. Copyright 1943 by T. S. Eliot, renewed 1971 by Esme Valerie Eliot.

George Allen & Unwin for material from *The Religion of Man* by Rabindranath Tagore, 1956. *The Buddha's Way* by H. Saddhatissa, 1971.

Macmillan, London & Basingstoke and Macmillan Publishing Co. Inc., New York, for lines from *Gitanjali* by Rabindranath Tagore, 1913.

Methodist Publishing House, London, for verses from the *Methodist Hymn Book*, 1933 Edition.

New American Library Inc., for material from *Sayings of Confucius* edited by J. R. Ware, 1955; Lao Tsu's *The Way of Life* edited by R. B. Blackney, 1955.

Oxford University Press (Oxford and New Delhi) for lines from *Three Plays* by Rabindranath Tagore, 1950; *Science and Christian Belief*, 1955; the World's Classics Edition of Dante's *The Divine Comedy*, 1932; Oxford University Press and Cambridge University Press for verses from *The New English Bible*, 1970.

Penguin Books Ltd., London, for permission to use material from: *Bhagavad Gita* translated by Juan Mascaró, 1962. *Buddhist Scriptures* translated by E. Conze, 1959. *Encounter with Martin Buber* by Aubrey Hodes, 1972. *Only One Earth* edited by Barbara Ward and Rene Dubos, (Andre Deutsch), 1972. *Plato: The Republic* translated by H. D. P. Lee, 1955. *St. Augustine: The Confessions* translated by R. S. Pine-Coffin, 1961. *The Early Church* (The Pelican History of the Church) by H. Chadwick, 1967. *The Fall* by Albert Camus, 1963.

Rafael Buber, Jerusalem, for permission to summarise passages from *The Knowledge of Man* pp. 76-77 and *Between Man and Man* p. 20 by Martin Buber.

Random House, New York, for material from *The Wisdom of China* by Lin Yutang, 1949.

Sheldon Press for material from *The Search Within* by C. Humphreys, 1977.

Viking Penguin Inc., New York, for material from *Buddhist Philosophy in Theory and Practice* by H. V. Guenther.

A. P. Watt & Son, for lines from *The Chinese* by Winifred Galbraith, 1942.

Wildwood House Ltd., London, for lines from *Tao Te Ching* by Lao Tsu translated by Gia-Fu Feng and Jane English, published in Great Britain by Wildwood House Ltd., London 1973. Reprinted by permission.

Preface

The subject of this book may be introduced by several justifiable assumptions. Knowingly or unknowingly people of all races and cultures are engaged in a perpetual search for social and spiritual liberation. Because of this common experience it is probably at the level of spirituality that philosophies and religions may meet without compromising their several traditions. It is at this deeper level that the concept of the hidden way emerges and it ought to be pursued because it will have a salutary effect on the multi-racial society which is our present inheritance. Every new discovery in this direction and every effort that is made to reap the practical benefits of these discoveries will help to ensure a future of peace and understanding. The hidden way must be seen as a joint enterprise between man and his Maker. According to the prophet the Lord said, "I will make a way in the wilderness" (Isaiah 43[19]), so the way is initiated by the Lord himself. But his servants have a responsibility also, "In the wilderness prepare the way of the Lord" (Isaiah 40[3]). Thus were laid the foundations of the way which underlies and undergirds those formal expressions of it which have emerged in the long pilgrimage of man. Revelation and response, inspiration and intuition, vision and obedience, guidance and virtue, instruction and experiment, are essential elements in the formation of the hidden way.

"It is impossible", said the Roman Senator Symmachus in one of his debates with Saint Ambrose of Milan, "that so great a mystery should be approached by one road only." It is certainly true that God does not leave himself without a witness in any part of the world. There are many ways to spiritual reality and inevitably people aspire to it along different roads. They come humbly and adoringly, and we recognise that the seeking and finding are not confined to any single race or culture. The following pages show that in different parts of the world — in China, India, the Middle East and the West — the search is fundamentally the same. Sometimes liberation is found through a deeper understanding of the natural world as in Taoism, sometimes through the practice of meditation as in Hinduism, sometimes through a process of gradual renunciation as in Buddhism, and sometimes through believing and practising the way of reconciliation as in Christianity.

The Greeks used an interesting word which may further our understanding. The dromos was a track or course on which certain unforgettable events took place. The dromos also referred to the race of life itself as when St. Paul said, "I have finished my course". Whether in Greece or Egypt or Rome the dromos invariably led to a shrine. The shrine symbolised the liberation and enlightenment which signified the purpose and culmination of life's quest. Perhaps the dromos and the hidden way are the same. What a striking difference it makes to an individual's aspiration and outlook when he realises that the way he is travelling and the ancient dromos coincide! Was there a dromos at the Good Will Corners section of Grindstone Village where, according to tradition, Confucius met and received new light from Lao Tzu? Can it be that the dromos crossed 'the field of Truth on the battlefield of life' where Krishna's words of wisdom changed the outlook of Arjuna: "The unreal never is: the Real never is not". (Bhagavad Gita 2[16]). Maybe on that full-moon night of May the Buddha found himself walking on the dromos in a deer park near Banares. Certainly the holy truths which characterise his message came to him as he walked that road of destiny. And have we not heard of the Damascus dromos where the great apostle saw a light from heaven which changed the direction of his life?

No one who has travelled such a road will be unaware of its effects. But the awareness carries commitments which can never be denied. This hidden way has no geographical limits, no cultural boundaries, and no lines of racial demarcation. It is the one primeval, universal way, divinely planned and traversed by the saints of every age and place. Indeed, any traveller who has become aware of its permanent features — harmony, wholeness, serenity and reconciliation — is already on the hidden way which leads him to his real destination.

My thanks are due to the members of the Book Club, Woriur, Tiruchirapalli, where representatives of different Faiths met month by month. Even though our differences were not suppressed, there was a recurring feeling that each of us was treading a path not entirely unfamiliar to the other. The Apostle's words rang true: "In every nation he that feareth him, and worketh righteousness, is acceptable to him". (Acts 10.^{35}). I wish to thank also the Kadans in the Anamallai Hills who, in hacking a way through the jungle and rediscovering an ancient track, planted the germ of an idea which has taken some time to fructify. I am grateful also to the young people in Lynchburg, Virginia, who told me that they hoped one day to find a way where their culture caught up with their vision. Perhaps they had a gut feeling that there existed a seminal way where these two could be brought together. Nor ought I to overlook the debt I owe to the students in my Adult Education classes who have questioned and cross-questioned my ideas till at least some of them have become crystallized and presentable. I am grateful also to my colleagues in the clergy courses whose interruptions: "Hold on", "Not so fast", "Will you spell that?" "Will you say that again?" have often had a salutary effect. "Good on you, brethren" for keeping the reins fairly tight, but not too tight to restrict the freedom of my explorations within the generous confines of the hidden way. My thanks are extended to my publisher whose personal interest in the subject is expressed in the meticulous attention given to the production of this book.

Introduction

We are always on our way somewhere. We are never still. Even at this moment, whether we are doing something or nothing, we are on the move. In imagination or in thought, in fantasy or in memory, in the things we desire or the things we fear, we are on our way. Our becoming explains our being. Exiles in this world, and what noble mind from Euripides down, has not had this feeling? Yet we only know that we are exiles because we think we belong. Even our alienation presupposes our destination.

So many of our great classics are about people going on journeys. The Odyssey, The Divine Comedy, Pilgrim's Progress, The Ancient Mariner, Moby Dick, The Kon-Tiki, are all journeys where discoveries transcend destination. They are important for a vital reason: the explorer explores himself. He may be convinced that there is an objective and a destination to be reached, and that there is a particular way to reach it, but these things may be less important than the reactions and intuitions, the uncertainties and hopes of the one who makes the journey. This is simply to say that the inward journey is more significant than the outward one.

The truth is that people all over the world are looking for some sort of way. The Hindus have accepted the principle that there is no single way that is appropriate for everyone. They speak of the way of wisdom, the way of meditation, the way of action, and the way of devotion. These are different ways which the soul has to travel to find union with Brahman. The purpose of life for the Buddhist is to travel the Holy Eightfold Path, the various stages of which are characterised by philosophical, moral and spiritual truths. It is a path which requires the strictest discipline, for sometimes it involves doubt and sorrow as it did for Gautama himself. But since man learns his duty step by step, it is a long and arduous way. As the ultimate aim is the extinction of all desire, victory is attained only after the fiercest mental and spiritual struggles. It is a way for those not easily daunted by difficulties, for those who have the stamina to endure to the end. For here again, our becoming explains our being.

The central concept of Taoism is the Tao or the Way. It is the supreme excellence. It is beyond description, for if you think you can define it, you have obviously not understood it. While it is the driving power in all nature, it also has to be discovered by all people in the varied experiences of life. The Tao is the controlling force in the universe and also in human life, the second because it is the first.

There are four aspects to the Islamic way: the way of submission to Allah, the way of unity which is attained through obedience to the Shari'a, the way of Sufi mysticism, and the pilgrim way to Mecca.

Christianity was originally thought of as a way leading to life, and Christians were those who were "of the way" (Acts 9.2). It was also thought of as a way of love. When Paul wanted to guide the Christians in Corinth out of their factions and jealousies, he said: "And now I show you the best way of all". (I Cor 12.31), and the way is outlined in the following chapter. In answer to a question from Thomas, Jesus replied: "I am the way; I am the truth and I am the life". (John 14.6). So the questions that cry out for an answer are: Why is it that many of the world's religions use the concept of the way? How is the way to be interpreted in each religion? How will the answers to these questions affect us today in a multi-racial society?

The Taoist Way

The Idea Of The Way As Interpreted In Taoism

The Music of the Spheres

The Universe in relation to Man

The Five Basic Elements

The Ritualistic Significance of the Five Elements

The Philosophical Significance of the Tao

The Qualities represented by the Five Elements expressed in Chinese Society

The Music of the Spheres

Although the world is composed of a multiplicity of things, it is still a universe and not a multiverse. There is one law or principle which runs through all things. This unity produces harmony and it is in harmony with this cosmic principle that man finds his highest good. Such is the basic truth of Taoist philosophy. Originally there was a Great Turning Point or Ultimate from which came two modes of activity, Yang and Yin which represent the forces of energy and inertia, light and darkness, maleness and femaleness. From the interaction of Yang and Yin came heaven, earth and man. These in turn were influenced by the Five Elements each of which played a dominant part in changing the seasons of nature, characterizing the items of creation, and effecting movements in the world of heaven, nature and man. This belief in a rational cosmic order to which rulers and subjects must passively conform in the interests of peace and welfare, has characterized Chinese thought from earliest times. The preoccupation with "the music of the spheres" is prominent in oriental thought. India has been inspired with the same theme. Tagore even compares creation with the making of a musical instrument: "The fire is lighted, the hammers are working, and for laborious days and nights amidst dirt and discordance the musical instrument is being made. We may accept this as a detached fact and follow its evolution. But when the music is revealed, we know that the whole thing is part of the manifestation of music in spite of its contradictory character".[1] Tagore quotes O'Shaughnessy to imply that man's poetry and imagination are significant contributions:

> *We are the music makers,*
> *We are the dreamers of dreams.*[2]

This may be one reason why man receives an artistic importance in eastern thought which is virtually unknown in the west till the Renaissance. In Taoist Philosophy man forms a sort of trinity with heaven and earth, and his mind is the master. This is why man is sometimes called a microcosm of the universe. Yet sometimes the same theme is echoed in the west:

> *You are the music*
> *While the music lasts.*[3]

Music implies balance and harmony, movement and rhythm, action and rest, and these were the terms in which Chinese thinkers understood the development of the universe. A static, unchanging universe was not for them. Although all things were in a state of flux, a pattern might sometimes be discerned. Like a kaleidoscope, in movement it presents a dazzling if impressive mystery, in stillness it produces new symmetrical designs. In the same way, for the Taoist, movement was the instrument of change. The Yang-Yin theory with its action and reaction of opposites is rather like an ancient version of the theory of electrons. Yet the main interest of early Taoists was not scientific but ethical. Their minds were firmly set in the paths of ethical thought and they believed that all things must be related to their ethical and social meaning. They examined the past rather than contemplated the future. Their aim was to examine things as they had been rather than explore the nature of things they did not know. They would not have appreciated the Hindu prayer: "Lead us from the known to the unknown", that is, from the things we know to the things we do not know. But they would have understood St Paul's words: "All things work together for good" (Rom 8.28). Taoism is the attempt to restore to human beings their original and natural goodness.

The Universe in relation to Man

One of the extraordinary things about Taoism is the strong connection between the physical structure of the universe and the qualities which characterize human civilization. It is unusual to link the physical composition of the world with those human qualities which are necessary for the preservation and understanding of it. It is sometimes said that the Tao is indefinable but even that is in some sense a definition. And as we have only words with which to understand it, we must use them in the hope that they are not too impoverished to shed some light. The Tao is a cosmic, dialectical, physical and metaphysical principle that pervades all things. Cosmic since it is coextensive with the world, dialectical since it works by the impact of opposites, physical since it produces the five elements, and metaphysical since according to Chinese thought it results in those five qualities which constitute civilization. The chief way of understanding the integral unity behind this concept is meditation.

The theory of Taoist meditation is based upon a view of man as a microcosmic universe reflecting the macrocosmic universe around him. The movement of the inner and outer worlds is intimately correlated. Outwardly man is influenced by, and indeed is part of, the vast forces of heaven and earth. Inwardly also he follows their universal pattern. His physical functions have cosmic analogies. His heart beats to a certain rhythm, his breathing is rhythmical, he dances to a rhythm and if he is fortunate, his voice produces music and rhythm. It is from cosmic analogies that the Taoist system of meditative breathing is constructed. Through such breathing man achieves the natural integration of self with the universe. By pursuing this idea of universal identification the Taoist achieves harmony of the microcosmic universe within and harmony with the macrocosmic universe without.

The Five Basic Elements

The macrocosm is composed of five basic elements: wood, fire, earth, metal, and water. All these are linked with the Tao and cannot function without its influence. The Tao serves man like a living, growing, fruit-bearing tree; like the sun whose unceasing energy sustains the world; like the good earth which provides a home for all creatures; like metal which art turns into beauty and industry into machine tools; like water finding its own level and fulfilling its function humbly, without fuss or praise. So even the five elements serve as instruments of the Tao. Nor is this all, "Man himself being an integral part of nature, was also the result of the interplay of these cosmic forces. They constituted by their interaction and harmony the life-force within him. The same forces, working in human history take the form of cycles which issue in the development of society, morality and civilization".[4]

Wood is the first element. Pictures by Chinese artists invariably include a tree, and those that do not are noticeably more western in design. It is not simply that a tree is beautiful, it is indispensable. The Sung landscape painters would feel that the scene was incomplete without a tree. This is not surprising for is it not true that a tree provides man's basic needs: shelter, food and health? A tree is man's best servant providing fruit, beauty, shade, herbs to cure his diseases, beams for the building of his home, and materials for the demonstration of his art.

Wood produces fire. In Chinese thought fire represents energy, light and permanence. Fire, associated with divine energy, is an early concept in many religions. In the Vedic religion of India, for instance, fire was the first-begotten of the gods:

That One by force of heat came into being.

Like the smouldering fires of a volcano the cosmic energy is never still. The sun or the fire is the source of all energy and perpetually sustains all living things. It is hardly necessary to draw attention to the mysterious powers that lightning and the sun have exercised over man and nature. Sometimes fire is used in the mystical sense as the first principle of all things, the eternal light of which all other lights are merely reflections. This is why mystics of different ages and faiths will re-echo Dearmer's words:

> *The heroes and the saints*
> *Thy messengers became;*
> *And all the lamps that guide the world*
> *Were kindled at thy flame.*[5]

Although this refers to the celestial fire, it is also closely linked with the warmth, fire and zest in the Yang principle which is regarded as a symbol of human energy.

Earth is the third element. The energy to which we have referred sustains the planet on which we live. Yet it is strange how man has assumed that no limits may be set to his exploitation of the earth. The dangers of this false assumption have been high-lighted by the Stockholm Report 'Only one earth'. It is impossible to miss the wistfulness as well as the challenge of these sentences: "Alone in space, alone in its life-supporting systems, powered by inconceivable energies, mediating them to us through the most delicate adjustments, wayward, unlikely, unpredictable, but nourishing, enlivening and enriching in the largest degree — is this not a precious home for all of us earthlings? Is it not worth our love? Does it not deserve all the inventiveness and courage and generosity of which we are capable to preserve from degradation and destruction and, by doing so, to secure our own survival?"[6] It is now, though late, widely recognised that the earth should not be overworked or turned into a dust-bowl, or denuded of its natural and aesthetic assets, or turned into a concrete jungle. At the heart of this ecological problem is man's failure to distinguish between his wants and his needs. Yet this recently-found western interest in human environment is not new, it is implicit in the ancient teaching of the Tao. For Taoism has always had a positive approach to this question. The earth is sacred and good but it is also subjected to an intricate network of interdependent laws which demand and deserve respect. Failure to show this respect even in a single instance, may produce indescribable devastation. This is not an appeal to return to nature, but to turn to nature, learning its lessons, understanding its laws and respecting its life-giving powers. Earth provides man with a suitable environment in which he may grow and thrive, giving him a home and providing for his varied needs. As he has graduated to an advanced civilization, one element has proved indispensable and that is metal.

It may fairly be claimed that metal has played a more important part, both positively and negatively, in the development of civilization, than any of the five elements. Its value is seen in silver and gold. Its variety of uses has produced outstanding human achievements. Its combination with other substances to form alloys has made it more malleable and durable as well as making it capable of fulfilling many different functions. It is the greatest single contributor to the astonishing developments in a technological age. Moreover, it is uniquely represented by the perfection of the bronze figures and decorative sacrificial vessels of the remote Shang dynasty of ancient China. In both past and present it has been the instrument of man's remarkable scientific and artistic triumphs.

Water, the fifth element, represents the ideal human disposition and is symbolic of China's strong ethical outlook. Indeed in Chinese thought the qualities of water are often applied to human beings. Water finds its own level, adapts itself to its surroundings and seeks out the lowest places. Yet water holds a power unknown to more solid and brittle things. It ignores frontiers and dividing walls, and functions by being itself. The oceans of the world unite continents and make possible communications between nations. Not only do the seas provide vast amounts of food but also are used in gigantic industrial projects. As omnipresent potential energy it is without parallel in the whole universe. Humility and power: the first is the secret of human excellence, the second the dynamo of industrial progress. When these five elements are closely examined there is little wonder that Chinese thinkers were inspired not only to make them the basis of a philosophy of the nature of the universe but also a philosophy of man himself.

The Ritualistic Significance of the Five Elements

Each of these five elements has a ritualistic application. Ritual is the link between the universe and human behaviour. Wood is the first because it symbolizes the basis of Chinese culture. Used in a variety of ways wood becomes mankind's healer, protector and beautifier. The tree becomes man's protector and healer and in this way ought to symbolize man's attitude to the poor and needy. For just as he is protected by the wood used in the building of his home, so he must in turn give care and protection to the aged and helpless. He takes his lessons from the tree. From wood he creates patterns for his bronzes and plaques on which he portrays images of the great ones of the past. The sensitivity, imagination and respect which are expressed in his art must also be shown in the pattern of his life, in his care for the young and his courtesy towards all. His art is also the art of life. It is for these reasons that wood is regarded as the basis of Chinese culture and civilization. To learn the ordered way of doing things man must show respect to the aged, assistance to the weak, guidance to the young and courtesy to all. These qualities are implicit in the first element.

Fire is represented by the sun which gives order, regularity and rhythm to the seasons of the world. It is this order which helps to draw out from human nature all that is true and beautiful. Nature impresses man by its regularity and reliability and he in turn reflects these qualities in his attitudes and relationships. A man becomes correct in his attitudes and values when he takes the trouble to cultivate the correct attitude towards nature. His obedience to the rituals becomes a recognition of his respect for nature's instructions. Ritual therefore serves as an instrument to form a man's character. Orderly ritualistic action is an expression of order in the universe itself.

It is not always realised that as early as the first century B.C. Tsou Yen put forward the theory that the earth was of spherical shape, perhaps the first rejection of the flat earth theory. He was regarded as a dreamer of dreams which is not surprising when it is remembered that he propounded his theory fifteen hundred years before Copernicus. In Chinese thought the round earth symbolizes completeness and harmony; it is the eternal mandala. So the earth in its wholeness and harmony represents the recurring mandala in human dreams. There was a primeval harmony and it is man's principal role to recapture it. He is made aware of this harmony in music and in the fulfilment of his duty; that is by hearing and doing. Although the earth is the third element it is also the central one. It is called 'Heavenly Nourisher' because it sustains and unifies the other four elements.

Indeed, the whole Taoist concept presupposes a close interlocking relationship between an elaborate philosophy of the natural world and the practical requirements of day to day religion.

While it is true that metal has brought many dangers to mankind, there is no doubt that when forged into tools and machines, it has also brought economic and social freedom. Nor is it an accident that the names of metals mark the ages and stages of his progress. So much of his advancement has been due to his inventiveness in the use of available metals. The modern age is important partly because it signifies man's mastery of technological skills. The freedom which metal has brought him is the freedom to use more fully his creative powers. But man requires another freedom: he needs to be set free from himself. Chinese philosophers have not been unmindful of this other freedom. Careful observance of his social and religious obligations neutralizes man's over-awareness of power and sets him free from the egotism which, if unchecked may destroy him. In these ritualistic commitments his thoughts are projected to the Will of Heaven, to the requirements of his family, to reverence for his ancestors, and to the spiritual as well as the social needs of his community. He knows how to act correctly and courteously and courageously, and these are the marks of a free man. To desire what is good for all is freedom.

Water has an even more striking connexion with human character and conduct since it epitomizes the qualities of man. More remarkably, in the Tao Te Ching water is several times compared with the Tao itself, the highest honour. It functions unobtrusively, humbly, and yet possesses great strength.

> *The highest good is like water,*
> *Water gives life to ten thousand things and does not strive*
> *It flows in places men reject and so is like the Tao.*[7]
> *The softest thing in the universe*
> *Overcomes the hardest thing in the universe.*
> *That without substance can enter where there is no room,*
> *Hence I know the value of non-action.*[8]

> *Under heaven nothing is more soft and yielding than*
>   *water,*
> *Yet for attacking the solid and strong, nothing is better;*
> *It has no equal.*[9]

Similarly if a great king is self-effacing and strong, he will be a stabilizing influence in the world. His object will be peace which means that families will be secure on their land and the people will be thoughtful, kind and honest. Society must be protected from tyranny, anarchy and war, and this is possible only if the qualities symbolized by water are exercised. There was an ancient belief that the planet maintained its equilibrium because it floated on the oceans of the world. The life of the family and nation are held steadily on the ocean of duty and obligation. So while these five elements are real, constituting the very structure of the universe, they are also symbolical of the way China has developed artistically and culturally through the centuries.

The Philosophical Significance of the Tao

Having considered the origin of the five basic elements and their connection with the ritualistic practice of man, we must now explain how the Tao became the focus of religious and philosophical ideas in China. The Tao is the centre of cosmic unity. It may be regarded as an emergent synthesis to which everything in creation is ultimately directed. It is the goal of the whole process of creation.

> *The one far-off divine event*
> *To which the whole creation moves.*[10]

Yet the way forward is also the way back for it is a return to the source of all things.

> *Primal virtue is deep and far,*
> *It leads all things back*
> *Towards the great oneness.*[11]

The following verse makes it clear that there is a still centre
which holds all things in balance.

> *The ten thousand things rise and fall,*
> *While the Self watches their return;*
> *They grow and flourish and then return to the source,*
> *Returning to the source is stillness which is the way of*
> *   nature.*[12]

Here then is a cosmic unifying ideal, the alpha and omega of the
universe. Western thinkers have been influenced by this aspect
of Taoist teaching. In 'Pointing the Way' Martin Buber describes
the teaching of the Tao as "the path towards a life of unity and
harmony", and although Buber later regarded it as "a stage that
I had to pass through before I could enter an independent relationship with being", it is certain that many people find even
this transitory stage too difficult to attain.[13]

C. G. Jung also was led to a similar truth. His book on
'Psychological Types' brought him to the conclusion that every
judgment made by an individual is conditioned by his personality type which makes every point of view necessarily
relative. "This", he says, "raised the question of the unity
which must compensate this diversity, and it led me directly to
the Chinese concept of Tao".[14] But this was not merely a phase,
as in Buber's case, it was the crucial factor in his psychological
journey. "It was only after I had reached the central point of
my thinking and in my researches, namely, the concept of the
self, that I once more found my way back to the world".[15]
Both Buber and Jung travelled on the journey of self-realization
and both took some of their directions from Taoist teaching.
And where did they find the secret of the highest state of man?

> *Those who know do not talk,*
> *Those who talk do not know;*
> *Be at one with the dust of the earth,*
> *This is the primal union.*
> *He who has achieved this state*
> *Is unconcerned with friends and enemies,*
> *With good and harm, with honour and disgrace,*
> *This therefore is the highest state of man.*[16]

The Tao is also the criterion of action. That is to say it provides a standard of action more reliable than the words of a virtuous ruler. A ruler may be influenced by external factors, the Tao will be influenced only by itself. A ruler may be unpredictable, the Tao never. A ruler may change his mind, the Tao is unchangeable. A ruler may be inconsistent in his administration of justice, but constancy is the mark of the Tao. A ruler will die, the Tao is immortal.

Therefore the Tao is independent of and superior to any government. The Tao holds all things in true balance. It is superior to the law in that the law calls for a minimum standard of conduct. For example, the law says, "Thou shalt not kill", but this is a far cry from the positive requirement to make every effort to preserve life, to spread happiness, and to show mercy and forgiveness.

> *I have three treasures which I hold and keep;*
> *The first is mercy; the second is economy;*
> *The third is daring not to be ahead of others.*
> *From mercy comes courage; from economy comes*
>   *generosity;*
> *From humility comes leadership.*[17]

These three treasures prompt the correct attitude to enemies as well as friends. In this way the Tao outshines the secular law.

The Tao has a positive role too: it links an individual life with the cosmos. The individual is thus able to see himself in historical perspective as well as in terms of natural oneness. The Tao imparts to life a spiritual quality which brings equanimity and tranquillity. This equilibrium in turn brings a sense of liberty and spontaneity. Yet behind all this is the need to find detachment and this is the hardest lesson of all.

> *In the pursuit of learning, every day something is acquired,*
> *In the pursuit of Tao, every day something is dropped;*
> *Less and less is done until non-action is achieved,*
> *When nothing is done, nothing is left undone;*
> *The world is ruled by letting things take their course,*
> *It cannot be ruled by interfering.*[18]

These are severe words to non-oriental ears. Life without striving or fretting, the willingness to lose rather than gain, the idea that non-action may have its rewards, are notions that are difficult to believe. To be sure the pressures of western life and the activism of western thought do little to encourage such passivity and detachment. But perhaps the greatest form of learning is to unlearn, and to stand at a distance and assess what is really happening may teach us that to do less is sometimes to achieve more. It may be wise patiently to wait and look and listen, and let things take their course. In any case, the opposite syndrome provides no cure. Fretting and fuming under life's pressures blurs the vision so that we cannot see which way to take.

> *Late and soon,*
> *Getting and spending;*
> *We lay waste our powers.*[19]

Stillness, a serenity born of patience, is required if ever we are to find out whether a purposeful and deliberate way can be traced or whether we are engaged merely on a random exercise.

Knowledge of the Tao sets the spirit free. For in the end Taoism is a plea for freedom of mind and spirit. On some occasions in history it has been a protest against the harmful and artificial effects of over-organization, stereotyped ideas and regimented behaviour. Consequently, the traditional and some-times fossilized attitudes of Confucianism have been seriously challenged. Life, spontaneity and freedom are key concepts for the Taoist, and its appeal partly lies in allowing other people and other communities to be free. The first necessity is to allow this freedom to the universe itself. Man is asked to respect nature because it sustains, enriches and enhances human life. There is also the implicit belief that nature will lead man aright. Nature's harmony is to be found not by exertion but by inaction, not by rebellion but by acceptance, not by dominance but by co-operation. It finds its own equilibrium if left to itself, and so will human nature. The forces of war, violence and aggression will be nullified since they will be denied opposition. Tranquillity, therefore, will be substituted for chaos. The secret of contentment is hard to find but it must be found. How? The real way is to submit to the forces of nature without any striving, to learn how to act without exertion, to see a unity behind a multiplicity of things, and to wait quietly and patiently till the highest knowledge is revealed.

> *Fame or self: which matters more?*
> *Self or wealth: which is more precious?*
> *Gain or loss: which is more painful?*
> *He who is attached to things will suffer much,*
> *He who saves will suffer heavy loss,*
> *A contented man is never disappointed.*[20]

There is a sense in which the Tao is man's greatest friend. In the divine scheme of things there are three important factors: heaven, because that is the source of all things; earth, because that is the complete environment of man; man, because his life and destiny are made possible and shaped by heaven and earth. All things are directed to one end, that man should understand the meaning of his existence. The Tao provides the conscious element in man whereby he in turn apprehends the Tao. For the Tao is the faculty which understands, the invisible guide leading man through his earthly life. Those who are wise co-operate with the Tao in making the world perfect in beauty and happiness. They will not debase or destroy any part of creation but preserve and improve it. What is the result of this co-operation between the Tao and nature and man?

> *Not putting on a display,*
> *They shine forth;*
> *Not justifying themselves,*
> *They are distinguished;*
> *Not boasting,*
> *They receive recognition;*
> *Not bragging,*
> *They never falter . . .*
> *Be really whole,*
> *And all things will come to you.*[21]

Of course it would be foolish of man to destroy nature when all things are going his way. But if he has no knowledge of the Tao, how does he know "all things will come to you"? It is, in fact, the Tao which harnesses the mighty forces of nature so that they serve human ends. The Tao gives constancy to nature and if this constancy which controls and inspires all the manifold operations of nature became the controlling characteristic of human nature, what would be the result?

> *Knowing constancy is insight,*
> *Not knowing constancy leads to disaster;*
> *Knowing constancy the mind is open,*
> *With an open mind, you will be open-hearted;*
> *Being open-hearted, you will act royally,*
> *Being royal, you will attain the divine;*
> *Being divine, you will be at one with the Tao;*
> *Being at one with the Tao is eternal,*
> *And though the body dies, the Tao will never pass*
> *away.*[22]

Silently and unobtrusively the Tao guides nature in the service of man. In one impressive line we are told:

> *It fulfils its purpose and makes no claim.*[23]

But supposing man has desires which nature cannot satisfy, needs of which nature is ignorant, what then?

> *Why does everyone like the Tao so much at first?*
> *Isn't it because you find what you seek*
> *And forgiveness when you sin?*
> *Therefore this is the greatest treasure of the universe.*[24]

There is the secret. The reason why the teaching of the Tao was so widespread in ancient times was because it offered forgiveness. The Tao is honoured when sinners are forgiven. Man's forgiveness consists in the fact that he will never be lost in the world, and will feel at home in it. Ultimately, nothing can harm the man who is identified with the Tao.

We began by considering the five basic elements — wood, fire, earth, metal and water. Then we discussed how the five ritualistic practices — culture, order, harmony, freedom and

stability — emerged from these basic elements. Then we discovered that the connecting link between them was the Tao,
the centre of cosmic unity. We must now illustrate how these
five qualities are woven into the texture of Chinese society.

The Qualities represented by the Five Elements expressed in Chinese Society

Culture

The tendency in China has been to look to the past for the
Golden Age rather than to the future. The idyllic age is often
described as the Grand Harmony or the Great Learning. The age
is sometimes thought of as a legendary era when the Emperor
Yao ruled in splendour. At his accession all the people said:
'Blow out the candles, the sun is up'. Again the Golden Age
may refer to the astonishing artistic achievements of the Shang
Dynasty. In any case, it was always assumed that the remote
past held secrets which succeeding ages longed to know.
Confucius clearly thought that he was the appointed custodian
of the tradition of the past. 'Since King Wen died, is not the
tradition of King Wen in my keeping or possession? If it be the
Will of Heaven that this moral tradition should be lost, posterity
shall never again share in the knowledge of this tradition. But if
it is the Will of Heaven that this tradition shall not be lost, what
can the people of K'uang do to me?'[25]

Hope is kept alive by maintaining continuity with the past.
For it is precisely by preserving the sacred tradition that the
Grand Harmony may be recaptured. New factors do not render
the old answers inappropriate but only serve to underline the
need for traditional values. Tradition had already confirmed
these ancient values, and they must be humanised and internalised in each new generation. Chinese culture endorses Goethe's
words:

> *What from our fathers*
> *We have inherited,*
> *Must first be earned by us*
> *If we would have it.*

Despite alien domination, cruel tyrannies, and centuries of imperial extravagance, the Chinese people have never lost this reverence for their past. It is partly, however, in the homespun wisdom of the villages that many of the ancient traditions have been preserved. In proverb, story and song, the past lives and sways the present. Even the radical changes of the past thirty years will be viewed as a scene in a theatre in which the real China will be able to make itself known. Modern leaders have been brought up on village folklore which does not lose its appeal. For instance the proverb: 'To understand earth, you must have known heaven', means that it is impossible to understand life's horizontal dimension which includes loyalty, reciprocity and sincerity, without knowing the Will of Heaven. For even if Chinese people appear to be reluctant to use the word 'God' in the singular, they do not hesitate to use the phrase 'the Will of Heaven'. The phrase is sometimes used interchangeably with the Tao. The source of all things becomes their mother; find the mother and you will know the child. The Tao is the ultimate mother of all, real in the sense of being the mother of all things, reliable in the sense of being unchanging, resilient in the sense of being the centre of growth, reticent in the sense of fulfilling her cosmic purpose constantly and unobtrusively.

This knowledge of the Will of Heaven inspires compassion towards those in need. 'I grumbled because I had no shoes till I met a man who had no feet'. Even to repeat this proverb prompts the altruism of the next saying: "I am not concerned that man does not know of me, I am concerned that I do not know of him'.[26] Tenacity is needed if ever these ideals are to be translated into everyday action, and tenacity is one of those qualities which have been essential in rural China. It was said of Confucius, "There is a man who is undertaking something even though he knows it can't be done".[27] Some of these proverbs have no doubt inspired village people not to lose sight of the ideal of freedom however remote it might sometimes have seemed to be. 'The silk-worm weaves its cocoon and stays inside, therefore it is imprisoned; the spider weaves its web and stays outside, therefore it is free'.[28] Such sayings characterise the

culture of the Chinese village representing consecutively compassion, altruism, tenacity and freedom.

These qualities and many more were in evidence in the days
of their great ancestors. 'At this time when men followed the
Great Way, all under heaven was owned in common. Men were
chosen for their ability and talents. Their teaching was reliable
and they cultivated harmony. People of ancient times treated
not only their nearest relatives as relatives, and not only their
own children as children. They cared for the aged until the end.
There was employment for the strong, and the young were
given opportunity to grow up. Widows, orphans, invalids, and
those left on their own were all provided for. Men had their
work and women their shelter. They accumulated provisions
because they did not wish anything to be thrown away, but
they were not permitted to amass goods for themselves. They
toiled because they did not wish goods to be anything but the
result of their own efforts. But they were not permitted to do
this for personal advantage. Therefore selfish schemes did not
arise, and robbers, thieves and rebels were not in evidence.
They went out without shutting the door. This was called the
Great Community'.[29] It may be that distance has lent enchant-
ment to the view but it is a noble statement and any nation
would be proud of it whether as a memory or a vision. Is it
possible that the days of the Great Community may return?
It may be possible. We live in a vast spiritual universe of which
the invisible world is an integral part. It is invisible because
we lack the necessary perception to see it. But this ability will
come as our minds are properly attuned and expanded. A few
are able to perceive that spiritual universe but.only because they
are beings of immense intelligence, love and spiritual splendour.
These are able to appreciate that extra-dimensional realm. These
intelligences are angels and archangels, the spirits of saints and
sages of the past who co-operate with the Tao in guiding the
world in its progress towards ultimate reality. There are also
lower spirits which are neither good nor bad, but when
offended by human beings, they may do untold harm.
Occasionally, however, a person may be so identified with the
Tao that he is regarded as a custodian of its powers. One or two

virtuous Sung Emperors were described in such terms.

Some of the Sung scholars might have qualified also for they were certainly extraordinary men. Such a man was Chu Hsi, the twelfth century scientist. The originality of his ideas is striking. He claimed that matter was neutral and must be made to serve the good. He differs from Greek and Hindu philosophers who believed that matter was evil and actively hostile to the good. Traditionally China has held fast to the notion that all things serve the good but the good must be reclaimed and re-interpreted by succeeding generations. Like the preacher in Ecclesiastes Chu Hsi believed that there was nothing new. The new was merely a reappraisal and re-understanding of the old. Man's aim was to find the universal reason which becomes obscure and must be explored in every age. All men possess a knowing faculty; at the same time there is a reason for every-thing that exists. The spur of all science is to bring these two together. The incompleteness of our knowledge is due to the inadequacy of our investigations into the reason for the exist-ence of things. If this is put right, the day will come when all things will become clear and intelligible. No wonder Shao Yung thought that to be human and Chinese was a great boon. With these twin blessings he might be the one to bring together the individual mind and the universal reason. 'I am happy that I am a human and not an animal, a Chinese and not a Barbarian, and that I live in Loyang — the most wonderful city in the world'.

One of the reasons why the Chinese have maintained interest in continuity and tradition is because it leads to the stability of human character. Individuals are not puppets or automatic toys. Since they are self-conscious, reflective beings they ought to be respected. Emphasis on tradition deepens this respect. Those values and customs are preserved which are worth preserving.

This does not mean, however, that tradition is never modified. New factors are taken into account and the past thirty years of Chinese history are clear evidence of this. New ideas and ideals are tested, and if acceptable, become internalised. It is natural that man should adopt principles which will ensure his future. He can never contemplate his disappearance with equanimity. Generally he chooses principles which are rational and ethical, and these prove to be functional as well. Evil is a failure to strive, anger a failure to think, and inhumanity a failure to love. If he cultivates real values, he will be able to create order in his own life and in the community in which he lives.

Order is a vital concept in Taoist thought because it is believed that everything in human life ought to reflect the order in the natural, external world. If there are no collisions in the universe, it is because all things operate in mutual compliance. Mystics are revered because they cultivate the qualities of compliance, forbearance, tolerance, mildness and self-abnegation. An ordered life is the first step towards an ordered society.

In considering this concept of order we must introduce the Chinese doctrine of the li. It is not easy to define because it is in itself a way of life. In general it means that whatever is deemed to be our specific duty should be performed at the appropriate time, in good taste and in good order. The original meaning of the li is connected with the sacred vessel in which offerings were made to ancestral spirits. But the vessels used to honour their ancestors were also used to feast their friends. This close association between the living and the dead is of considerable importance, for those who honour the dead are most likely to respect the living. The sacrificial idea penetrates every aspect of Chinese life. The ancestral temple or shrine is a sort of sacred inn. It is traditionally the meeting-place for business transactions and discussions about social problems. All important considerations and decisions should take place in the presence of ancestors. It follows that the temple was a rendezvous of life, not of death.

Now the word 'li' came to be applied not only to business transactions but also to religious ceremonies. The correct observance of these ceremonies was a sign of good conduct, and the word came to mean 'that which is done correctly'. A man's character and relationships, his business life and religious duties were governed by the concept of the li. This life-style meant that man's actions were motivated by a pattern of selfless, co-operative attitudes. He was expected to discharge every trust as if he were assisting at a great sacrifice.

Indeed, the man who lives according to the li takes right as his principle, reduces it to practice with all courtesy, and renders it perfect with sincerity. If he has faults, his sincerity is tested by his willingness to correct them. If he perpetuates his faults, he is insincere. To see what is right yet not to do it is not only cowardly but false. Magnanimity is one aspect of sincerity, it involves doing more than is expected without seeking any reward.

Moreover, the man who lives according to the li is always courteous. The custom of bowing is not merely a formal matter but a sign of deep respect for others and reverence for sound tradition. Courtesy is the visible expression of moral uprightness. If people do their duty in a courteous and orderly manner, it will lead to a compassionate and orderly society. A man is courteous because he recognises the worth and uniqueness of another person. So if we were to describe a man who embodies the cardinal virtues of Chinese life, we would say that he is a man who is impartial in his relationships, who seeks justice for all classes of society, who is honest in public administration as well as in private affairs, and who has respect for the value of personality.

The good life is something to be treasured. It is the ideal for all citizens. It is the only fully adequate life since it schools a person to meet all contingencies. It is unaffected by success or adversity. The key to the good life is reciprocity which underlines the concept of the li. The following passage from the Book of Rites shows how the idea of order penetrates every aspect of Chinese life:

'The ancients who wished to illustrate virtue throughout the kingdom first ordered well their states. Wishing to order well their states, they first regulated their families. Wishing to regulate their families, they first cultivated their persons. Wishing to cultivate their persons, they first rectified their hearts. Wishing to rectify their hearts, they first sought to be sincere in their thoughts. Wishing to be sincere in their thoughts, they first extended to the utmost their knowledge. The extension of knowledge is by the investigation of things'.

'Things being investigated, their knowledge became complete. Their knowledge being complete, their thoughts became sincere. Their thoughts being sincere, their hearts were then rectified. Their hearts being rectified, their persons were regulated. Their families being regulated, their states were rightly governed. Their states being rightly governed, the whole kingdom was made tranquil and happy'.[30]

We come now to the third element, the earth. From the ritualistic point of view it is the eternal mandala. It symbolizes completeness and *harmony*. This idea of harmony is an important and integral part of Chinese thought. It pervades every aspect of life, philosophical, religious, and social. When the Yin and the Yang are joined together they form a circle. This is no accident. All opposites are embraced in the circle which is the symbol of harmony and final unity. Life is not like a straight line moving onward and upward towards a final pinnacle; rather it is like a revolving wheel which moves one way and then the other but never stops. Like a spiral staircase, it never moves far from the centre.

The purpose of the li is to create harmony. Courtesy if not regulated by the li becomes laboured effort; caution if not regulated by the li becomes mere timidity; courage if not regulated by the li becomes unruliness; and frankness if not regulated by the li becomes mere effrontery. Many ceremonies in China are accompanied by music, for music expresses harmony of character as well as harmony of sound. The Greeks had the same notion. Aristotle said: 'Music has the power to form character; and the various kinds of music may be distinguished by their effects on character'.[31] Plato goes even further: 'Rhythm and harmony penetrate deeply into the mind and have a most powerful effect on it'.[32]

It is the poets in China who skilfully link music and nature.

> *Deep in the bamboo grove sitting alone,*
> *I play on my lute and sing a lone tune,*
> *There is no one in sight*
> *Save the moon glittering bright.*[33]

It was said of Tao Yuan Ming that 'he was drunk with the fumes of Spring'. He tells the story of a poet who lost his way in the creeks of a river. Slowly he pushed his boat through a dense grove of peach trees and suddenly before his eyes was the Taoist Utopia. It was a beautiful village, quaint, simple and remote. It was a place where nothing more could be desired.

> *Wealth I want not, honour I desire not,*
> *Jade palace is beyond my dreams;*
> *Then let me enjoy the happy hours,*
> *And stroll in the garden among my flowers;*
> *I'll mount the spring hill and sing my songs,*
> *I'll see the clear brook and verse my poems;*
> *Ah! by course of nature all fade into infinity,*
> *Whence comes my anxiety?*[34]

There is a story about Wang Fu who, while staying in the capital, heard one moonlight night a man playing a haunting melody on a flute. It filled him with joy and he painted a picture of bamboo and stones. In the morning he went to see the player in order to present him with the picture. The man was a cloth merchant and gave to the artist a fine red carpet and asked him to paint another picture to make a pair. This made Wang Fu so angry that he took back his picture and tore it to pieces. How could it be repeated? How could he recapture the initial inspiration? As for the carpet-seller, the haunting melody had been overwhelmed by the harsh dissonance of the market-place.

Perhaps nature has found a harmony which eludes man. Nature moves easily to its own harmony. It represents things that live and grow, change and mature in beauty. All this is not merely an occasional episode but a continuous process. Sunrise, sunset; new moon and the moon at the full; Winter and Spring; ripening buds and falling leaves, illustrate the varied rhythm of life itself. Will man ever find the harmony which nature expresses? Li Po gives a clue:

> *Why do you dwell in the mountains?*
> *A rude man questioned me;*
> *I laughed and did not answer,*
> *The river flows down to the sea;*
> *My soul is in my own keeping,*

In flower is the red peach tree;
My earth and heaven beyond other men's grasp,
And what is that to thee?[35]

Nature's harmony is heard by those who wish to hear. According to Fan Kuan of the Sung dynasty the purpose of existence is to discover this harmony. One day he woke up and sighed to himself, 'The men who came to see me yesterday have never tried to seize things as they really are; for surely things themselves are better teachers than men, and the heart is a better teacher still'. So he retired to the hills and lived among rocks and rivers and trees. He spent his time studying the affect of clouds and mist, of wind and moon, and of darkening and clearing skies. In the silence of his soul they spoke to him, till his brush could express their inmost meaning. To see things as they really are; to seize things as they really are; to portray things as they really are; this was his quest. His only sadness was that he might fail to enable others to hear the hidden melodies and find the hidden way.

One of the principal themes of Chinese thought is the 'art of the heart'. This means the use of art in spiritual development. It is assumed that by birth man possesses balance and fitness. But he may lose this balance through acquisitiveness, anger, grief and calamity. Positive qualities help to restore the balance. Music is good because it neutralizes grief. Poetry is good because it gives comfort in sorrow and provides the light of vision in dark moments. Ritual is good because it elevates to a richer dimension everyday things. Music and ritual restore life's equilibrium. So harmony remains and imparts a needed rest.

The Tao of earth is that which is at rest. At rest because acquisitiveness is checked, and discord and disunity are banished. Only when this happens is harmony attained. From harmony comes tranquillity. Listen to the wind, it is the flute-music of heaven. The great breath of the universe carries music to our ears. So nature gives what man must learn to hear and live by. This paves the way to *freedom.*

It was said earlier that the producing and shaping of metal had brought out the artist in man. Perhaps it brought out the religious enquirer as well. Creativity sets the spirit free and in this way art serves religion. Freedom of worship is one of the characteristics of religion in China. There are community temples in which several deities are lodged in one place. These deities may be the Earth God, the Jade Emperor or the Queen of Heaven. Mostly, however, they are ancestors who have been promoted to the status of deities. Those who have had disappointing and disillusioned lives are more likely than others to attain a divine status. Just as negative forces are eventually neutralised by the results of piety and worship, so a life which appears to have failed, despite its virtue, will be raised to a higher plane after death. In some community temples the sages are honoured too. In the early days of the Boxer Uprising it was customary to have a banner on which a sage was drawn. Above his head were three haloes, and the inscription read:

> *I am the Buddha of the cold cloud.*
> *Before me is the black deity of fire.*
> *Behind me is Lao Tzu himself.*

Although these were used as political slogans, they are in fact religious symbols. The Buddha represents peace; Confucius, the black deity of fire, represents zeal, and Lao Tzu represents fulfilment. The symbol for the last is the river of destiny. In modern times popular worship in China centres on the community temples.

The festivals which celebrate nature are also of religious significance. The balance of seasons produces the right balance in the earth. Everyone must have a right relationship with the earth, for nothing can prosper without this. Indeed, without the fruit of the earth there is nothing to celebrate. Those people are wise who have learned to work with the earth, and not against it. Those are wise also who have the patience to believe that wisdom will prevail when society needs it. This happy state will be brought about through good government, law and order, and respect for the powers of nature. There is a general assumption in China that if men of noble disposition rule China, the nation will experience peace and prosperity. Tu Fu of the T'ang dynasty sums up this truth:

Great heaven unkind
Is sending down these miseries;
Let noble men come to rule,
And rest the people's heart;
Let noble men do justly,
And the evil day depart.[36]

The man who rules virtuously will be in harmony with the Tao.
Yet those who are ruled have an obligation as well. The Book of
Rites is explicit on this truth: 'The duties of universal obligation are five, and the moral qualities by which they are carried
out are three. The duties are those between ruler and subject,
between father and sons, between husband and wife, between
elder brother and younger, and those in relationship between
friends. These are the five duties of universal obligation.
Wisdom, compassion and courage — these are the three univer-
sally recognised moral qualities of man. It matters not what way
men come to the exercise of these moral qualities, the result is
one and the same. Some men are born with the knowledge of
these qualities; some acquire it as the result of education, and
some acquire it as the result of hard experience. But when the
knowledge is acquired, it comes to one and the same thing'.[37]

It is a man's duty to alert his family to its obligations. One
of the great family occasions is when ancestors are remembered.
The Chinese firmly believe that it is a good thing in life's zenith
to remember its end. Remembering the dead also implies a
renewal of life, for the winter of Yin is followed by the spring
of Yang. Every funeral is another reason to venerate ancestors.
A priest is essential to see that everything is done in the traditional manner. The whole celebration becomes a drama. Careful attention is given to the presentation. Nothing must be left
to chance. The robes and shrine and the spoken words must be
exactly as prescribed. An effigy of the person who has died will
be placed upon the shrine. A beautiful mansion is produced
which has been lovingly cut out from cardboard. It is a reminder
of the splendid habitation which the lady will receive in the next
world. The lady's soul is at present in limbo. The priest reads a
pardon and immediately her soul is released. Since her soul is
now elevated to its true habitation, the cardboard model is

burned. The priest now calls for the aid of divine spirits to drive out all diseases and bring eternal bliss to all the worshippers. It should be remembered that death creates disharmony by upsetting the balance of life itself. Funeral rituals heal the breach which has been made by death. In this way the desired harmony is restored. The key to the whole ceremony is the Writ of Pardon which is read in public by the priest.

From all this we learn that Taoism rejects dogmatic and inflexible interpretations of religion. Freedom implies liberty of worship and liberty of interpretation. A man must be free to co-operate with the gods, with nature, and with his ancestors. Religion is the fulcrum which holds in balance the forces of Yin and Yang. In order that this fulcrum may function properly men must fulfil their obligations, serve the gods, revere the powers of nature, and venerate their ancestors. Sometimes magic and superstition play a part in Taoist ceremonies, and charms, relics and amulets are sold at shrines. However, these, are aberrations from true Taoism and not of its essence. It is therefore erroneous to suggest that while Confucianism satisfies the philosophical seekers, Taoism appeals to the credulous and superstitious ones. The foregoing pages have attempted to correct that mistaken attitude. Taoism is a noble attempt to interpret man's understanding of the universe and of the moral and spiritual forces which influence his individual and communal life.

We have already noticed that water, the final element, is most closely associated with the qualities of character — humility, *stability* and contentment. The best way to understand this is to examine the qualities which are expected in the life of a sage. The sage is the custodian of divine wisdom. He keeps to the Tao teaching and is an example to the world. He attains this wisdom through knowledge, intuition and meditation. He is virtuous but self-effacing. He fulfils his role without fuss or ostentation. Yet others perceive his worth because of what he is. He does not parade his knowledge. He does not wish to compete with those who think they know more, so others do not envy him or try to injure him. He is humble and retiring in disposition and therefore remains entire. He does not insist unfairly on his own point of view. He possesses honesty, integrity and a quiet and steady faith. He does not fuss or worry or frantically rush around. In ordered meditation he arranges his affairs, then patiently awaits the outcome. If the hallmark of his character is inaction, it is inaction based on inward confidence.

The sage is an example to others. He does not thrust on others his unasked advice. He guides by warm goodwill and simplicity. He does not overwhelm his friends by referring to his lofty ideals. Rather he will invite them to an intimate meal, listen to their problems, and by sharing ideas, will impart his peace. His demeanour dissuades them from engaging in foolish or rash actions. People learn from him without realising it, and this is called instruction without words. If he is head of state, he governs so lightly that people hardly notice it, and because he is not burdened with ambition, his people live in simplicity and contentment. A verse from the Tao Te Ching emphasises this truth:

> *If the sage would guide his people, he must serve with*
> *humility,*
> *If he would lead them, he must follow behind.*
> *In this way, when the sage rules, the people will not feel*
> *oppressed;*
> *When he stands before them, they will not be harmed.*
> *Because he does not compete, he does not meet*
> *competition.*[38]

Now we must consider the sage as the ruler of his people. Because of the ruler's tranquillity, the people lose their fears. The sage does not rule by the imposition of laws. Nor does he pile up punishments for every crime. People who live in constant fear may seek to live a good life for the wrong reason. The sage wants his people to be joyful as well as to feel secure. So he applies two methods which are better than laws: information and partnership. People are not left in ignorance about what the ruler is seeking to do. Knowing his plans, they become more and more responsible. The sage rules in partnership with his people and both rise or fall together. He possesses authority

so that he may not have to wield it. He leads without flamboy-
ance.

Above all, the sage is a practical philosopher. He teaches his
people that if a man wishes to be identified with the Tao, he
should discard all prevailing notions about life and nature, and
observe things for himself. 'Be vacant and you will be full.'
By this he means that they must begin where they are, not seeking to be someone else or somewhere else. Heads are so cluttered
up with preconceived ideas, pet theories, prejudices, intolerant
attitudes, and false knowledge, that it is better to discard it all
and start afresh. Emptiness leads to fullness. At least, whatever
is gained will be the result of personal choice. The task is
uncommonly difficult but it also has uncommon results.

> *Yield and overcome;*
> *Bend and be straight;*
> *Empty and be full;*
> *Wear out and be new;*
> *Have little and gain;*
> *Have much and be confused.*[39]

If man observes things for himself he will learn nature's
secrets. He will notice that where there is light there is shadow,
that short is derived from long, that water seeks the lowest
place, and beauty shines in all circumstances. All phenomena
have a dual aspect and the source of all is the Tao. By over-
coming ambition, avarice and pride, and by entering into the
rhythm of nature, the greatest boon of all is achieved — contentment. The sage who constantly teaches his people how to attain
this is indeed identified with the Tao.

References

1. Rabindranath Tagore, *The Religion of Man*, Unwin, p. 10
2. *Ibid*, The poem quoted is 'The Music Makers' by A. W. E. O'Shaughnessy, p. 77
3. T. S. Eliot, *Four Quartets*, Faber and Faber, p. 44
4. D. Howard Smith, *Confucius*, Temple Smith, p. 112
5. P. Dearmer, *Methodist Hymn Book*, No. 279.4
6. B. Ward & R. Dubos, *Only One Earth*, Penguin, pp. 298-9
7. Gia-Fu Feng & Jane English (Trans.), Lao Tsu's *Tao Te Ching'*, Wildwood House Ltd., ch. 8
8. *Ibid*, ch. 43
9. *Ibid*, ch. 78
10. A. L. Tennyson, *The Works of Alfred Lord Tennyson*, Macmillan, p. 286
11. Lao Tsu, *Tao Te Ching*, ch. 65
12. *Ibid*, ch. 16
13. Aubrey Hodes, *Encounter with Martin Buber*, Penguin, pp. 181-2
14. C. G. Jung, *Memories, Dreams, Reflections*, Fontana, p. 234
15. *Ibid*, p. 234
16. Lao Tsu, *Tao Te Ching*, ch. 56
17. *Ibid*, ch. 67
18. *Ibid*, ch. 48
19. W. Wordsworth, *Longer Poems of William Wordsworth*, J. M. Dent
20. Lao Tsu, *Tao Te Ching*, ch. 44
21. *Ibid*, ch. 22
22. *Ibid*, ch. 16
23. *Ibid*, ch. 34
24. *Ibid*, ch. 62
25. Lin Yutang (Ed.), *The Wisdom of China*, Random House, New York, p. 247
26. J. R. Ware (Trans.), *Sayings of Confucius*, Mentor, I.16
27. *Ibid*, XIV.38

28. Lin Yutang (Ed.), *The Wisdom of China,* Random House,
    New York, p.506
29. W. H. McNeill & Jean W. Sedlar (Ed.), *Classical China,*
    (Passages are from 'The Great Learning'), Oxford,
    pp. 45-51
30. *Ibid*
31. G. Lowes Dickinson, *The Greek View of Life,* Methuen,
    p.149
32. H. D. P. Lee (Trans.), *The Republic of Plato,* Penguin,
    . p. 142
33. Arthur Cooper (Trans.), *Li Po and Tu Fu,* Penguin
34. R. Totewall & N. L. Smith, *The Penguin Book of Chinese
    Verse*
35. Winifred Galbraith, *The Chinese,* Penguin, p. 44
36. *Ibid,* p.19
37. W. H. McNeill & Jean W. Sedlar, (Ed.), *Classical China,*
    Oxford, pp. 45-51
38. Lao Tsu, *Tao Te Ching,* ch. 77
39. *Ibid,* ch. 22

The Hindu Way

The Hindu Way

The following headings which form the framework of this section are based on the 'limbs' or stages of meditation presented in Pantanjali's 'Yoga Sutras' in the third century B.C.

The Way of Restraint
    a) Reject violence
    b) Reject falsehood
    c) Reject acquisitiveness
    d) Reject self-indulgence
    e) Reject covetousness

The Way of Positive Action
    a) Purification
    b) Patient endurance
    c) Discipline
    d) Self-knowledge
    e) Attentiveness

The Way of Harmony

The Way of Breath-Control

The Way of Sense-Withdrawal

The Way of Concentration

The Way of Meditation

The Way of Enlightenment or Samadhi

The Way of Restraint

a) Reject violence

The first requirement is to refrain from doing harm to others. Ahimsa means harmlessness or non-violence. Although it is sometimes used as an instrument of political pressure, it is best understood as an inward disposition rather than external actions. If there is a protest, it should be one of soul-strength rather than brute force. It does not mean meek submission to the will of an evil-doer but the setting of the soul's spiritual power against the will of a tyrant. Its sole aim is not to damage another person in any way. Violence is wrong because it gives expression to base instincts. It accomplishes nothing construc- tive and merely creates more problems. Moreover, it presupposes that external, enforced discipline is more effective than inner, spiritual discipline.

Two of the great teachers of Hinduism during this century have been Mahatma Gandhi and Rabindranath Tagore. Three virtues were paramount in their message: truth or moksha, non-violence or ahimsa, brahmacarya or chastity. Reverence for life is the essence of the doctrine of non-violence and its source is the individual's experience of truth. Truth is therefore inseparable from non-violence and chastity. Positive and universal love requires self-restraint in all things.

If you stop at the gate of Santiniketan, the garden of peace, where for many years Tagore sought to apply the principles of his faith to everyday requirements, you will read this inscrip- tion:

> *The taking of life in this place is forbidden.*
> *The bringing of flesh or of any idol to this ashram*
> *is forbidden.*

Speaking slightingly of any duty is forbidden.
Indulging in unclean mirth is forbidden.[1]

If these are turned into positive virtues, they become universal love, the sanctity of labour, and purity of thought and action. Such virtues spring from an inward experience. The residents of Santiniketan are not just under a rule of life but under a rule of grace. Refusal to accept this rule of grace would not merely be an insult to the founder of the ashram but to the paddy-fields, the mango grove, the cows which provide food and the sephali bushes which provide the garlands.

Although the word 'forbidden' is used several times in the inscription, it should be correctly understood. Whoever wishes to enter Santiniketan for study, meditation and hallowed labour, will already have discarded those things which are a hindrance to truth, peace, love and purity. In this connection negation and passivity are too often misunderstood. Negation may mean doing nothing, passivity means deliberately eschewing aggression. Negation implies resignation, whereas passivity means that all ends must be attained by non-violence. Ahimsa never means that a person is powerless to alter a situation, on the contrary, it assumes that much can be achieved by spiritual power and moral influence.

It should also be noted that the karma theory assumes that the future can be shaped by good thoughts and actions here and now. Moreover, others benefit from such actions. Good actions have the resonance of musical notes. As Tagore says:

The light of thy music illumines the world[2]

Ahimsa should be seen as a protest against all forms of tyranny, that of caste, of imperialism, of so-called progress, but it is also an affirmation on the grounds of the ultimate efficacy of the love of God. It is only when the bonds of anger, hatred and revenge have been broken that there is freedom to love and forgive.

b) Reject falsehood

The next requirement is to refrain from falsehood. It is possible to be false to oneself, to others, to the highest we know, to God. The rejection of falsehood is the first step towards truth. Truth in this connexion should not be equated with the knowledge of a number of facts. It is not the kind of truth which can be tested simply by the value of its consequences. Nor is it the consensus of widely accepted ideas. Truth is inward light or spiritual attainment. To be true is to be genuine. To be true is to be, to be false is not to be.

The Hindu saints of the past sought God and truth through meditation. They reached the conclusion that these were one and the same, and it became customary in India to say not that God is truth but that truth is God. Man's duty is to reflect the light of truth. If he rejects that light, he is not left just as he was, he is definitely worse. All kinds of consequences follow from this rejection of truth. A man may deceive himself without being aware of it. He may make excuses saying that all are in the same boat so why be anxious about it. He may begin by hardening his heart only to discover that his heart is hardened. It is no longer a passing phase but a permanent state. If the situation is to be corrected, he must learn the lesson of contemplation.

One of the maxims of Hindu philosophy is that the mind assumes the form of that which it perceives. It follows that to apprehend truth is in some sense to become truth. It is sometimes suggested that such a concept is alien to western thought, yet we must not forget Aristotle's words: 'The thinking mind becomes its object in the act of comprehending it'. Hegel also echoes the same truth: 'In our highest thought, we reach potential identity with the divine'. But there is nothing quite so explicit as the Mundaka Upanishad III: 'He who knows Brahman becomes Brahman'.[3] The question is, however, how is the mind prepared so that it desires to become the thing it contemplates?

Another maxim of Hindu philosophy is that religion is a necessary bridge that takes us to the higher reaches of

philosophical thought. The concept of a personal divinity is one
that has to be surpassed in order to reach the Absolute. For
instance, many Hindu Gods may be subject to the law of karma
but Brahman is free. This is another way of saying that the end
of religion is the transcendence of religion. Religious forms may
be necessary until the perfect unity is attained. Not that Hindus
neglect religion, far from it, but they know that the supports of
religion serve their purpose in so far as they bring us to a level
of consciousness which renders those supports unnecessary.
The soul is always saying: 'That which I seek is not here and
not there', so the search must continue until truth is attained.
Perhaps this is what Wordsworth meant:

> *The gross and visible frame of things*
> *Relinquishes its hold upon the sense,*
> *Yea almost on the mind itself, and seems*
> *All unsubstantialized.*[4]

c) Reject acquisitiveness

If refraining from violence and falsehood are the first and
second requirements, refraining from acquisitiveness is the third.
Perhaps more than any other virtue this one has characterised
the attitude and lifestyle of the typically ascetical Hindu. It
implies being satisfied with few necessities and not being
envious of the possessions of others. The serenity of the wandering sage who has renounced all is well described by Tagore.
The saint stands ready for his last journey:

> *I have got my leave. Bid me farewell, my brothers!*
> *Here I give back the keys of my door – and I*
> *give up all claims to my house . . .*
> *Ask me not what I have to take with me there.*
> *I start on my journey with empty hands and*
> *expectant heart . . . The evening star will come*
> *out when my voyage is done and the plaintive notes*
> *of the twilight melodies be struck up from the*
> *King's gateway.*[5]

It is axiomatic of Hinduism that the way of contentment lies through renunciation. The importance of this act of radical renunciation should not be underestimated. All the external trimmings of life are regarded as of no value for only holiness is worth the effort of mind and will. Honours, riches, titles and rewards are mere toys lightly to be cast aside.

Here is a genuine attempt to free human life from those external props on which it often rests — security, social conventions, success and the approval of others. Even if this Hindu pattern of life is formidable, it is not illogical, for the man who possesses nothing does not fear loss, and to be delivered from such fear is to find contentment.

Such an attitude fosters tolerance towards others, allowing them to be themselves and not seeking to draw them into a common pattern. Each must be allowed to follow his own path. The attempt to squeeze all types into one dogmatic path serves only to squeeze all out of the path of charity. Ultimately, the way of renunciation is a discovery rather than an attainment. Life is not striving to win a race but the realisation that there is no race. The fact is that as long as the will to win is dominant, the acquisitive and aggressive forces of desire are still active. However, the ideal in Hinduism is reached only by him who has no desires. His aim is 'to noughten all else', that is, to make it nought. This is the way to liberate the mind from its finite fears and anxieties. Where these obstacles are removed, the way is open for infinite qualities, one of which is contentment.

d) Reject self-indulgence

The fourth requirement is a protest against self-indulgence. It calls for a rejection of anything in excess whether it be eating, drinking, sleeping, or engaging in different forms of pleasure and recreation. Indulgences may mean the refusal to recognise necessary restraints. It is necessary to see these apparent prohibitions in the light of the Hindu idea of salvation or moksha. The most obvious effect of moksha is that it turns all life into an expectation. Nothing is just what it appears to be and life's possibilities are not as closed as they sometimes seem. The hope that characterises Indian thought, therefore, is different from that of the West. In the West the emphasis tends to be on triumph over the powers of evil which is necessary because of belief in man's original Fall. Or sometimes the 'triumph' emphasis refers to victory in the class struggle which is endemic in an acquisitive society. Such an interpretation makes hope identical with triumph and is viewed in contrast with the evil that pervades life.

Over against this the Hindu idea of hope is built on an expectation of salvation that pervades the whole of life. It assumes that life has never been wholly marred by radical evil so the quest for salvation is not a struggle leading to triumph but a patient determination to remove the husk which hides the kernel of truth. With the fear of evil removed, the nagging self-doubt, which cripples hope, is removed. When the concern with triumph is absent, there is no need to crush the opposition in order to realise the future. The secret lies in recognising the goodness of nature both in intention and achievement. Man's hope consists, not in triumphing over nature, but in accepting and revelling in its rhythms. The ray of light which he then sees will illumine the whole of life. Man's future is seen as a genuinely open one. This expectation releases man from the bondage of this world and transforms many of its events.

In order to reach this elevated state, the seeker requires a guru. Because the guru has been on a spiritual journey himself and is aware of the pitfalls and temptations, he is well equipped to lead someone else on the same path. First and foremost the guru is a holy man. He is also a teacher and counsellor. One of his skills is to realise that different disciples require different guidance. The guidance offered depends to some extent upon the temperament, education and spiritual response of the disciple. A guru will be a godly man whose moral reputation is beyond criticism. He will have a profound knowledge of the Vedas and Upanishads with a proven ability to expound their mysteries. He will have a wide cultural background and his acquaintance with poetry, philosophy and religion will extend far beyond the boundaries of his own faith. His gifts as a teacher will be paramount. He will discern truths that are important, lucidly expound their meaning, and relate that meaning to the disciple's condition and ability. Part of his task is to develop latent qualities so that growth in perception and wisdom may take place.

Above all, the guru keeps his main aim in view. He knows that life functions according to three principles: variety, harmony and unity. There is variety in the many faculties of the body, each part possessing a different function, yet each contributing to the work of the whole. The mind operates the principle of harmony and enables each part to serve the purpose of the whole. It is when each faculty works with and for the rest that harmony is produced. Unity, therefore, serves the purpose of harmony.

e) Reject covetousness

The last of the 'restraints' concerns the curbing of covetousness. Greed lies behind most of the sorrows and sufferings of the world. It brings poverty, injustice and resentment in its wake. So the grasping ego must be curbed. It is not easy for a young seeker to engage in a rigorous self-examination alone, for many questions may be evaded and some demands deliberately set aside. Here again the guru has much to offer. He will teach his disciple that there is no need to be preoccupied with an end-product. The end-product is the main concern of an acquisitive society. The use of a yardstick is inappropriate here. 'Pure awareness' is not something that can be demonstrated by saying 'I possess this', for in that moment it disappears. The real mystery is oneself and the ultimate aim is detachment. When everything else has been weighed, measured and balanced, and mapped out to scale, there still remains the 'self'. If this problem is evaded, all problems remain.

The self will always seek the ascendancy unless a person is taught the meaning of detachment. In communicating this meaning, certain important principles must be kept in mind. Not every disciple is at the same stage of intellectual and spiritual development. The temperament, interests and expectation of one person will be very different from those of another.

A good personal relationship between the guru and his disciple is vital. The wise guru will make his charge a subject for meditation. He will find out which approach wins a response and which does not. Are the responses prompted by fear? Are they suggested by someone else? Are the responses given merely for courteous reasons and are they given slowly, readily or ambiguously? It should always be recognised that the primary purpose is not to get the pupil to do something but to *be* something.

This is another way of saying that man is involved in a journey of self-discovery. Why is he so far away from his creative centre? Too frequently his soul is immersed in that which is alien to it. He seems to have drunk the waters of Lethe and forgotten his origin. He has to re-discover the still-centre of his being in face of the pressures of greed and covetousness. Solitude and silent meditation are necessary if this profound alteration in his being is to take place. Although the task is difficult, men seem impelled to seek this spiritual freedom. 'As the birds fly in the air, as the fish swim in the sea, leaving no traces behind, even so is the pathway to God traversed by the seekers of the spirit'.[6] Clear-cut answers are not forthcoming for each seeker must learn the lessons for himself. There comes a time when he is left alone, the teacher having done his part by inspiring the quest and pointing to the destination. Perhaps George Herbert comes close to Hindu thinking when he writes:

> *My hill was further: as I flung away,*
> *Yet heard a crie*
> *Just as I went, None goes that way*
> *And lives: If that be all, said I,*
> *After so foul a journey, death is fair.*[7]

The Way of Positive Action

We now come to the second phase of Patanjali's outline — the five observances or the ways of positive action. The emphasis here is not upon what must not be done but upon what must be

done. After the 'restraints' we have now a more constructive
programme. We shall begin with a typical Hindu story.[8]
Svetaketu, son of Aruni, went to the city of Panchalas and
appeared before King Pravahana Jaivali. The King asked, 'Do
you know how beings depart hence at death?'. The young man
answered, 'No Sir'. Then he was asked, 'Do you know the Way
of the Fathers and the Way of the Gods?' Again the young man
answered, 'No Sir'. The King told Svetaketu to find out the
answers to these questions. Hurriedly he went to consult his
father who could not enlighten him. On the way back to the
palace the young man met a holy man who instructed him to
'wait for the dawn, work till sunset, and watch for the fire'.

a) Purification

The first command means that enlightenment will come through
meditation. The second means that attention must be given to
karma for the Way of the Fathers is by practical action. The
third means that the wisdom that is sought will be found everywhere. This assumes that the seeker has eyes to perceive it. The
whole world of nature is alive with creative forces. Different
aspects of the created world are represented by the symbol of
fire. The sun is the fuel, the rays are the smoke, the day is the
flame, the moon is the embers and the stars are the sparks. It
is customary in Hindu households to offer an oblation to God
each morning through the kindling of the fire. This is also a
reminder that the fire of creativity and renewal is being offered
continuously by the whole world of nature.

Fire holds the secret of some of life's greatest lessons. It is
the source of energy, of light, and even of life itself. Agni, the
God of fire, was worshipped when men realised that the
elements of nature were not hurtful but creative and beneficial.
Fire is the symbol of purification as well as power. Man needs
to know what the world is so that he may understand its benign
and sustaining influence upon his life. The lesson to be learned
is that the energising force which animates the sun, the moon,
and lightning, is the force that indwells man, purifying and

transforming him. Even in Vedic times Agni, the divine fire, was expressed in triple form:

> *One in thy essence, but to mortals three,*
> *Displaying thy triple form*
> *As fire on earth, as lightning in the air,*
> *As sun in heaven.*[9]

Agni, the terrestrial deity, had a priestly function: as the sacrificial flame he carried the worshipper's prayer to the bright heaven; as fire on earth he was the homely companion who drove away the powers of darkness. The 'homam', the sacrifice made to fire, is a daily ritual which has been observed by Hindus from time immemorial. Fire brings everything in nature to a state of growth, maturity and perfection. Hence the description of what fire achieves 'as sun in heaven'.

b) Patient endurance

Following the symbol of purification, we now turn to consider the patient endurance which is necessary if enlightenment is to be found. It is at this point that the King's questions to Svetaketu are important. Souls are classified according to the measure in which they have acquired true knowledge, that is, have actually attained the knowledge which they sought. Souls in the second category are those that are dependent on ritual acts and moral works. The third category represents those who have neglected knowledge, ritual acts and morality, and have made no progress because of their indifference.

These three categories must be carefully noted because they lie behind the Hindu doctrine of karma. Souls that belong to the first group go, by the Way of the Gods, to blissful communion with Brahman. They go from light to day, from day to the world of the Gods, thence to the sun. From the sun they are led to the world of Brahman and from this blissful state there is no returning.

Souls that are still dependent on rituals and good deeds go, by the Way of the Fathers, to the moon. There they receive some of the consequences of their past existence whether these are felicitous or otherwise. Although this is a spiritualised explanation, these souls also become involved in the world of nature itself. They are symbolised by the smoke of sacrifice and pass from smoke to night, from night to the World of the Fathers, and from there to the moon. Then they return to the earth, passing from air to rain, from rain to earth, where they eventually become food. They are offered again in the altar fire which is man and born in the fire of woman.

Souls in the third group who, because of their indifference, have acquired no merit either by knowledge or devotion or good deeds, will continue on earth. They suffer for their neglect and indifference, but with greater effort and devotion, may eventually attain some higher form. Those who have ascended by the Way of the Gods have seriously sought enlightenment. Perhaps in several existences they have successfully overcome passion, illusion and ignorance. They are an example to those who are still toiling through their earthly existence and making little progress.

c) Discipline

Another way of constructive action is through discipline. Whatever view we take of the world, it is only through discipline that moksha may be attained. The world may be regarded as a domain of evil from which man must escape as soon as possible. The view that the world is enemy-occupied country is not typical of Hindu thought. A second possibility is to see the world as a testing-ground where men choose between good and evil. Hindus reject this because they think it puts too great a responsibility upon human beings and results in introverted and pietistical movements. One of the problems to be faced is that of disorientation. We are out of sorts, things are not holding together as they should, and we seem unable to analyse the causes of this conflict. Therefore a process of reorientation is needed. This involves restoring sense-control, orderliness of mind and spiritual discipline. These aims may be fulfilled through meditation.

The acceptance of discipline is paramount. The first thing to do is to be specific about time, place, correct posture and aim. Haphazard preparation leads to haphazard meditation. In the acceptance of discipline three requirements are necessary: an act of will, an act of submission and an act of faith. Failure in discipline is invariably a failure of will. Too often we are defeated at the first hurdle. So we must choose a time, a place, a lotus position, and a theme, and nothing must be allowed to interfere with this arrangement. To give the will a task is to honour and strengthen it.

Then there is an act of submission. Before we can be silent before the One, we must be silent before one, which means that we must be at peace within ourselves. Our mental sensitivities and spiritual energies need to be given the chance to be restored and replenished. Body and mind, spirit and will, conscience and feelings, all join in demanding that an opportunity for relaxation should be afforded. This act of submission means that our disordered and disorientated lives will become one and in their wholeness will be 'silent before the One'. These acts of will and submission need the support of faith. Faith in Hinduism implies action as well as belief. The devotee demonstrates his faith in many different ways: by going on a pilgrimage — possibly to Banares, by honouring the strict rules of meditation, by fulfilling a previously-made vow, or by accepting a commitment to sacrificial service. Faith is called in question if it is not demonstrable. These practical questions also involve his faith. Did you offer your gift at the temple? Did you walk round the temple an extra time? Did you fulfil the domestic rituals? Did you light the fire and did you wait for the dawn?

d) Self-knowledge

It is important to remember that study in a general sense is not enough. Self-study leads to self-knowledge, self-acceptance and self-direction. We have to recognise the ideal while facing the real. There are two tendencies in human nature: to attempt to adapt the ideal to life or to elevate life to the ideal. The first implies lowering the ideal and the second means leaving the ideal where it is and striving to attain it. The 'wayward angel' characterises the first tendency:

In my youth I set my goal,
Further than the eye could see,
I am nearer to it now,
I have brought it nearer me.[10]

If an ideal is placed before us and the first step towards reaching it is to forego self-interest, self-enjoyment and self-will, our tendency is to say that the ideal is impracticable. What we really mean is that it is too difficult to attempt. On the other hand, if we are presented with an ideal which can be reconciled with self-interest, we are brave enough to attempt it. Yet in the end it is the ideal that matters most. We must assume that divine truth can be attained. The Hindu maxim 'Thou art That' means that what we are and what we aim to be may be unified. The home of Atman, the individual soul, is Brahman, the Soul of All. To disbelieve in the ideal is to deny our true selves. The ideal can be reached and realised by everyone. The ideal becomes the real.

It is one of man's greatest assets that he inherits all that is good in the whole universe. This is what Emerson meant:

I am the owner of the sphere,
Of the seven stars and the solar year,
Of Caesar's hand and Plato's brain,
Of Lord Christ's heart and Shakespeare's strain.[11]

It is we who put our hands over our eyes and cry that it is dark. The ideal in which we believe and the reality which we experience is the discovery of our true nature. Everything else is false and an illusion. That is why we are bidden to become what we are. It is a matter of self-discovery. This discovery is made only after the most rigorous self-knowledge and self-criticism. Eventually the veil drops away and the soul's reality, in its purity and freedom, stands revealed.

e) Attentiveness

The last of these ways of positive action is attentiveness. Not attentiveness in a general way but awareness of the One. We cannot speak of two lives or two worlds, there is but one life, one world, and ultimately one existence in which all other existences are incorporated. Everything exists in that One. Men, animals, food and all created things are part of that One. Insofar as all creatures are included, all have the same value. Sometimes people become frozen in the snow or maybe in severe conditions the will to go on disappears, or perhaps they are overcome by sleep. Our nature is like that. In adverse conditions, we lose the will to continue, and hope slowly ebbs away. Is there an answer? We must keep awake. We must be fully aware of what is happening, and keep moving. We are on the Way and we should not allow adverse conditions to turn us from it.

In any case, attentiveness quickens faith. Faith in Oneness is the essential thing. It is not that doubt, fear and guilt disappear but rather that they are comprehended, included in the Oneness that is attained. Now everything that contributes to this fulfilment rings true. Hatred separates, love unites. Some things separate and destroy, love is the way to Oneness. This applies to thought too: if it makes for multiplicity and dis-integration, it is the wrong path; but if it unites and strengthens, it is the true way. If we feel for others, we are growing towards Oneness. When we accept all experiences without resentment or antagonism, we are nearing the fulfilment which we seek.

The Way of Harmony

In every area of life Hinduism stresses the importance of preparation. When the question is asked in India, 'What prepara-tions have you made?' it may refer to many different matters. For instance, it may refer to food, to the cleaning of the house, to rituals, to a pilgrimage or to meditation. Perhaps all the others culminate in the last. Everyone is expected to prepare his soul for its true destiny. A man must always be mindful of the way he thinks and feels, lives and acts. That is his karma. At the same time he must prepare for his true vocation, that is his dharma. To prepare himself adequately he must make the most of his guru. His guru is his instructor, counsellor and guide in a private capacity. All through his 'secular' years he is preparing himself for the 'forest years' when he will leave his home and family to live the life of a sannyasi, a man who chooses to become a hermit in the interests of holiness. In this way a man will give himself entirely to the life of prayer, meditation and renunciation.

However, it is wrong to differentiate too sharply between the secular years and the forest years because the practical preparation of a meal may be regarded as an act of devotion. A festival meal may take many hours to prepare, but hours are well spent in a labour of love. The lighting of the fire, the grinding and crushing grain into powder, the careful preparation of each ingredient, the time-honoured order in which these duties have to be done, all have their accompanying ritualistic significance. It may reasonably be asked why this meticulous attention is given to the needs of the body. It is the recognition that body, mind, spirit, conscience and will are of equal importance. The preparation of the whole being is one way of describing the function of meditation. Hinduism does not claim that the body is unimportant, merely that it is impermanent. In the cultivation of meditation the body is as important as the mind. Perhaps this is a lesson that the West has to learn from the East. It is essential to be on good terms with one's body because correct posture is part of the preparation for meditation. It is easy to say that meditation is possible in any place, at any time, but this is a misguided approach. Any time can easily become no time at all. It is surely desirable that some attention should be given to those methods and disciplines which feed the mind and spirit.

This does not mean that the body is regarded as a poor relation. 'Present your bodies', said the Apostle, 'a living sacrifice unto God, which is your reasonable service'.[12] The body is subject to very heavy demands. The car is serviced regularly to avoid trouble. In general the body is not so fortunate. The tempo of life is over-demanding. Mental stresses and strains inevitably cause physical strains. But ought the body to be subjected to unreasonable demands?

Part of the problem is that the body sometimes refuses to

do what the mind requires. The body makes its protest but the protest is ignored. Aches and pains, strains and tensions, are cries from the body saying, 'Enough is enough'. Sometimes the body declares a total strike and not without reason. When this happens, it is a serious situation for two reasons: it means that we have become insensitive to the body's limitations. In fact, we have allowed it to become a slave. It also means that we have unwittingly produced a sharp discord between the body and our non-physical faculties — mind, will, conscience and emotions. If the motor-nerves give way, there is no control over the movement of limbs. Something is needed to strengthen the control agencies. If nothing is done, there will be a civil war. Meditation is not only a control agency but a negotiating agency as well.

There is another problem. The discord thus created can rarely be localised, it pervades our whole being. Our minds and spirits have become a scene of conflict. The storm is raging and we have not discovered the art of silencing the storm. One thing is certain, we ought not to disregard the symptoms. We don't say, 'Only one violin string is broken, therefore it doesn't matter'. If one string is broken, it is impossible to produce the right tune. In order to resolve the conflict it is necessary not only to accept the limitations of the body but to alleviate the conditions under which it has to function.

The control of our body is our next concern. Why is the body given so much importance? There are several reasons: we can express ourselves only through the body. All the signals we make are made through the body. Nor should we think that the mind and spirit are confined by the body. On the contrary, the body is the medium through which the mind presents itself to the world. It can or should be a vehicle of freedom. It follows that sometimes the body is the vehicle of spiritual discipline. It may be involved in a journey, a pilgrimage, an act of sacrifice, a service of suffering. It needs to be strengthened in order to bear the strains of its immense spiritual tasks.

Again we have to remember that the highest trance and spiritual ecstasy are attained through the body. The body as well as the mind may experience great beatitude and complete calm. It is because of this realisation that the saints and sages are said, 'To touch the deathless element with the body'. And when the body is called a 'diamond' body, it is because of the infinite value of its spiritual achievement. These are some of the reasons why the control of the body is essential. Control of the body is necessary to enable the body to fulfil its spiritual mission. Control makes the body supple, steady and responsive.

The reason why correct posture is important is that it produces correct poise and balance and this is the result of harmony between different faculties. Meditation is the greatest single aid in producing this harmony. The body should be held steadily, with head, neck and back in a straight line. Two things are needed: the loosening of effort and the meditation on the Endless. This practice takes thought beyond the immediate, beyond obstacles and opposites. Little by little, posture becomes easy and natural. Gently and gradually the body learns to respond. This is summed up in the Gita: 'Let him find a place that is pure and a seat that is restful, neither too high nor too low, with sacred grass and a skin of cloth thereon. On that seat let him rest and practise Yoga for the purification of his soul: with the life of his body and mind in peace; his soul in silence before the One. . . .With soul in peace and all fear gone, and strong in the vow of holiness, let him rest with mind in harmony, his soul on me, his God supreme'.[13]

The Way of Breath-Control

It is unusual for any religion to expound a philosophy of breathing. Doubtless the therapeutic effects of correct breathing have been known for a long time but the connection of correct breathing with meditation techniques is an oriental emphasis. Yet it was a Hebrew wise man who said, 'The breath of the almighty giveth understanding'.[14] It is the symbolism connected with breathing that is important for the Hindu. A slow deep, rhythmic, regular inhaling and exhaling is an asset to meditation. Merely taking in air and releasing it does not fulfil the purpose of meditative breathing. The symbolism is along these lines: with an intake of breath an idea is sent on its inward journey. When inhaling, the idea sinks deep down; when exhaling, we bring the idea back from its journey. But when it returns the idea has gathered a richer meaning. The idea may return to transmit a feeling of elation or serenity. Or it may be that an interior satisfaction will pervade the whole of life. Again, following its journey, the idea may produce a moment of illumination, a needed spiritual insight, a half-forgotten truth, or awaken a memory from the past. It will enshrine a meaning which is significant for us.

It will now be realised that we are not merely describing breathing but an adventure of ideas. Of course we often refer to new ideas or fresh insights as due to inspiration which means the drawing in of breath. Not only does breath-control meditation presuppose an adventure of ideas but it also implies the transforming effects of these ideas. It may be argued that this will not lead to external revolution but it will lead to interior fulfilment.

There is, therefore, an intake of breath which brings purification and renewal to our whole being. Alongside this there is an intake of forms and ideas which derive added meaning and significance as they travel along the arterial ways of our bodies and the meditation routes of our minds. There may also be a suspension of sense-impressions which frees the mind from secondary activities and enables it to concentrate upon the subjects which it chooses rather than those which are chosen for it. There follows an inward harmony, for the received ideas are purified and our whole being is suffused with the concord and serenity thereby achieved.

At the practical level correct breathing is physically, emotionally, psychologically and spiritually beneficial to the individual. The practice of pranayana means the voluntary control of inbreathing, outbreathing and holding the breath. One of the advantages is that we become aware of what we are doing and why. When it is realised how many factors affect our breathing, we shall understand how important it is to be in control of the process. For instance, our breathing may be affected by fear, anxiety, resentment, physical exertion, room temperature or atmospheric pressures. It follows that the development of correct breathing may be used as a therapeutic measure.

Meditative breathing is similar to that of sleep — slower, deeper, quieter and more rhythmic than that of wakeful hours. We should aim therefore to create physical conditions which are conducive to successful meditation. This implies control of mind over body and will over mind. The idea is not to produce Olympic athleticism, although it may achieve that, but to create a balanced and healthy economy in the body. It is not enough to be satisfied with inferior habits of action or thought or emotion. In every area of life we need to exercise a wise orderliness and even times of relaxation require efficiency.

Sometimes it is necessary to prevent the mind from injuring the body. If the body is in a state of strain or tenseness, even concentration itself may be a burden to it. Sometimes the body needs to be rested, refreshed and revitalised. The Hindus have a saying 'There is no raja without hatha', which is another way of saying that there can be no advanced meditation, and the values which accrue from it, without relaxation in posture and correctness in breathing.

The purpose of correct breathing is to forget about breathing. We can forget the means when the end is achieved. It is not always realised that the soul grows by making bodily life a success. What is the artist doing? Is he producing a perfect picture or a perfect artist? What he becomes takes precedence over what he does. An inspired picture requires an inspired artist.

What are the beneficial results of practising meditative breathing? A bad habit is replaced by a healthy one. Loud, irregular and uncontrolled breathing is replaced by a smooth, rhythmic flow which produces harmony. Emotional disturbances are fended off which makes deeper meditation possible. The result should be mental and spiritual equilibrium. Serenity is attained as the mind becomes free from anxieties and our effective meditation will enable us to make an enlightened and positive contribution to the communal good.

The Way of Sense-Withdrawal

It will now be clear that the essence of the Hindu Way is chiefly concerned with finding ways of separating reality from illusion. Are there ways in which meditation can help us to achieve this? A description of the structure of the mind may help us here. In our minds there are receivers, a selector and a guardian. The receivers are in contact with the outside world. All impressions from outside are faithfully recorded by them. These outside influences may be thought-waves, sense-impressions, impulses, vibrations, and even a false self masquerading as the real self. In order to make any impact on the mind, these forces have first to pass the portals of the senses. It is necessary to establish some kind of control between the outside world and the mind.

We also possess a selector which sometimes accepts and sometimes rejects these impressions. Any impressions which are accepted are defined and classified. In other words, they are put into a form in which they can be handled. The third element in the structure of the mind is the guardian whose task is to keep control over everything that is taking place. The guardian endeavours to turn our experiences into knowledge so that they become part of our store-consciousness.

Now within every person there is an Atman — an individual soul — and everything must be done to prevent hostile forces from harming the Atman. It is one of the great merits of Hindu teaching that it shows in a scientific manner how the mind serves the soul. How is knowledge acquired? To a large extent it is acquired through our senses. Everything that we are or can be aware of is a product of two ingredients, the mental and the material. Some knowledge comes from within and some from the external world. Any movement from the material to the mental, from 'thing' to 'thought' involves the senses.

What exactly happens in the acquisition of knowledge? The forms or objects or events that we see on every side do not explain themselves. Any object that we see has a size, a colour, a consistency, a function, and a separate existence. Whenever we ask questions about it, we are making a transference from the material to the mental. Only when these objects are transmitted to the mind can they be described, assessed, categorised and quantified. The question is: how are external forms transmitted to the mind? How do we come to know the things we do know? All experiences pass into our awareness through the portals of the sense instruments — eyes, ears, nose, tongue and skin. We should know little of the external world if we did not possess these five senses. Let us consider 'sight' as the representative of all of them. We have the capacity to observe what is going on. The ability to do this does not belong to another wavelength but to our own. We can see what is going on and report it back to the mind.

However, all is not plain sailing; sometimes we look without seeing, listen without hearing, and speak without communicating. We suffer from these disabilities because we have not learned to use our senses properly. We need to find a way of minimising these disabilities.

Not only do we learn how to observe but we also learn that there is some correspondence between what we see and how we think and behave. This is true of all our senses. We are like radio receivers which are finely tuned. Receiving many impressions, we transmit them to our minds where they are carefully monitored. After external influences are observed and carefully checked, we draw certain inferences from them. We hear the music of a flute and it conveys great pleasure to us. We see a sunset and immediately appreciate its beauty. We touch a work of sculpture and find joy in touching it. All these pleasurable experiences come to us through the portals of the senses. But they are not the only influences which approach those portals. On the whole, our minds work efficiently but they have to deal with undesirable influences also. This requires a certain scrutiny, questioning, analysis, and sometimes even rejection. Now the difficult problem is: how much control have we over those impressions which are received by our minds through our senses? Is it possible to switch off the sense-impressions which we find unacceptable? Can we control our receptivity? Switching off the senses is called sense-withdrawal and there is no doubt that the practice of meditation is a considerable aid in attaining this control. If the mind is a transmission centre for all intake from the outside world, it must be trained to fulfil this purpose. It is required to select, reject, examine and despatch messages in all directions. Meditation prepares the mind for this onerous responsibility. Further, it prepares the body for the impact of sense-impressions, and engages the will to control the whole process. So meditation becomes an efficient regulator of the whole complex process of life. Without this there is invariably an haphazard routine which may result in disorder and disintegration. We have to decide for ourselves: do we desire an efficient routine, or one that is only moderate, or no routine at all?

We must now explain why an efficient routine is necessary. There are certain important principles at stake. The mind has to learn to discriminate. It requires the independence to say what it will or will not receive. If it is constantly overworked by dubious sense-impressions, evil impulses and false imaginings, it is in danger of being taken over by them. So its integrity must be maintained, it must be free to accept or reject. The more the mind is trained to approve of excellence, the more likely it is that this excellence will be reflected in every aspect of life.

There are occasions also when the mind needs to be completely detached from its surroundings, and to achieve this is one of the purposes of meditation. The mind has to learn the lesson of detachment before an individual can transmit the principle into everyday affairs. This is what Krishna meant when speaking of the devotee, he said, 'When he completely withdraws the senses from their objects, as a tortoise draws in its limbs, then his wisdom is firmly fixed'.[15]

Once the mind is released from its arduous routine duties, it is free for other tasks. This freeing of the mind is necessary because it gives the opportunity for creativity, inventiveness and new vision. The monotonous, everyday routine tasks may be so demanding that the real functions are relegated to a minor role. Sense-withdrawal then is the attempt to keep the thought-centres from receiving the impressions of the objects perceived by the sense-organs. If this work is done efficiently, it gives freedom to create, invent and contemplate.

The Way of Concentration

All that we have said about sense-withdrawal paves the way for
the next stage which is concentration. We have examined how
the mind functions especially in relation to the senses. It is
probable that the mind is sometimes surprised at the thoughts
it harbours. Concentration is an important function of the mind
but even here training is needed. In order to cultivate this gift
it is necessary to practise holding the mind to certain objects
and bringing it back again and again when it wanders. This may
be illustrated by taking it stage by stage:

    a. The mind concentrates upon one object — a point, a
line, a circle, an image or a scene.

    b. Our concentration must be such that our minds are not
affected in any way by other external events.

    c. We must be aware of the obstacles to concentration —
mental laziness, doubt, lethargy, clinging to sense-
impressions, and falling away from concentration once
it has been attained.

    d. We should be prepared to face the deprivations that are
necessary to maintain this experience. Silence, solitude
and fasting may be a small price to pay for learning the
profound lessons of concentration.

    e. Transcendental Meditation may be the outcome. This
means that the usual material aids are transcended. The
meditator therefore continues without the usual comfort and assistance of external aids. Physical conditions
are also transcended, for the mind is no longer troubled
by feeling, instinct, discomfort, or even by animation
and elation. The usual environment which may be
uncongenial, irksome and uninspiring, is also transcended. Not to remove these but to rise above them is the
purpose of meditation. Here is one of the ways of
suspending all outside influences — time, space and
location, and leaving only the object which the mind
contemplates. This is known as isolating the idea in the
inviolable circle.

Relaxation of mind is the precondition of such concentration. This is where the repetition of mantras, holy words or names or sacred sounds, will help. There is no need to engage in self-criticism or self-humiliation for this will detract from the relaxation of mind which we are seeking. All we need to do is to say certain words which, by their resonance, beauty and association, produce a detached habit of mind. Presently the chanting fades away and we find ourselves listening, listening when there seems nothing to hear. Perhaps the rhythmic lilt of the fading mantra still lingers, or perhaps we listen to the sounds in our own ears, or our own breathing or heart-beat. Or maybe the silence gives room for an interior voice which we have not heard before.

Let us suppose that we have selected a symbol for our concentration, the picture of a saint, a word, the red triangle of fire or the white circle of space. Let us choose the last. It becomes a circle of light. What does this mean? Our concentration produces a small point at the centre of the circle. Is this an indication to us that truth is at the centre? If we perceive this, we might also perceive that our lives are in the cosmic setting. We may find ourselves softly uttering a prayer of thankfulness, for the profoundest meaning of the experience is not what we are able to define or describe but what has taken place within us. And perhaps what has taken place is the realisation of the real, inner world. We have seen the white circle as the mandala of wholeness, the sense of integration, of peace and illumination. For once we see things as they are and not as they seem to be. Not as we want them to be or as we have been taught that they should be, but as they are. So the two worlds, inner and outer, become one.

It is axiomatic in Hinduism that certain words possess a sacred power. Such words are called 'mantras'. A mantra is chanted or recited as a preparation for meditation. Sometimes it is an esoteric formula which is not divulged to others. The mantra itself is a subject for meditation and is often addressed to Siva or Vishnu. Let us examine the sound 'OM' as this is one of the best known mantras. We shall refer to its sound, meaning, idea and spirit. The sound is a combination of the letters AUM. 'A' is uttered at the back of the mouth, 'U' in the middle, and 'M' at the front. The sound therefore is the epitome of all the vocal sounds. So this sound is thought of as the announcer of God. It is a synonym for the name of God. What does it mean? The three parts of AUM refer to the three Gods of the Hindu Trimurti: the 'A' stands for Brahm*a*, the 'U' stands for Vishn*u*, and the 'M' for Siva for he is often named *M*ahadeva, the great God. Other mantras may be limited in meaning but this one is all-inclusive.

What idea is embodied in it? It signifies the beginning, continuation and culmination of the work of creation. Brahma created the world but it was dead and motionless. So he called upon Vishnu to endue it with life. Brahma and Vishnu suddenly saw a huge pillar of fire and light which was personified in the form of Siva whose function is to destroy evil and wind up the affairs of the world. Sometimes they are called custodians of the created world, the living mind, and the spiritual purpose and destiny of the universe.

In India matters are often addressed to the three great Gods and the devotee becomes connected with them, sharing in limited ways their functions and powers. It will be noticed that in everything we do there is a material factor, a mental function, and an ultimate purpose. We exercise creativity in order to stop creating, having attained our aim; we think in order to stop thinking, having solved the problem; we live in order to stop living, for the schooling is over. Thus in saying AUM we become intrinsic partakers in the nature and function of the Trimurti itself.

The Way of Meditation

It is relatively easy for our thoughts to get out of control. They tend to follow what is sometimes called a 'tangential loop' and this makes it difficult to return to the main-stream of thought. Thoughts follow the line of least resistance or the line of habit. There is nothing wrong with this so long as we know what is happening and can change the routine if we wish to do so. The fact that it is natural to entertain wandering thoughts makes it all the more difficult to deal with them. Because one thing leads to another we think that it is logical but it may simply mean that we are following the easy path. Because it is natural, it is easy and before we realise what has happened, we are inveigled into day-dreams, fantasy, false imaginings and illusions. Such patterns become fixed in our minds and are regarded as part of the furniture. Just because we like a familiar, cosy arrangement, we allow the tangent to continue indefinitely. Why don't we try to correct this situation? Maybe we are too tired or have lost interest in what is happening. We just don't bother to stop the merry-go-round.

While all this has been taking place, our powers of concentration have become eroded and we must try to find our way back. By focusing on one thing we shall go a long way to solving the problem. The objects of our attention have become so diffused and diversified that they are hazy and indistinct. So it is essential to focus our attention steadily and consistently. Matters of colour, sound, shape and substance, will then be noticed much more sharply. The idea is to use all our faculties in order to attain this end. It is possible for us to see through the outward eye, the mind's eye, the eye of the imagination and the eye of recall. The latter means that we are able to see the object of our concentration when it is no longer visible to us.

During times of religious festivals most religions expect their adherents to practise 'instant recall'. The Hindu Dipavali, the Jewish Passover, the Christian Eucharist, and the Islamic Ramadan, are festivals during which an important event of the past is recalled. Although 'instant recall' means the ability to recapitulate an event, it also implies re-vivifying a past experience. To recollect the past may not mean that our present circumstances change, but our interior attitude may change. Hostile forces are kept at bay and have not power any longer to hurt the mind. Obstacles are transcended rather than removed. Sometimes people are referred to as 'dreamers', or 'lost in thought'. Actually detachment has sharpened their awareness. The great asset of this condition is that it frees the mind. Such freedom enables thoughts to take their own journey even though they are still under control. The mental range, therefore, becomes virtually infinite. To say that a man is 'lost in thought' may mean that mind transference has taken place. In this experience the mind is released from its limitations and starts its independent journey.

Sometimes we hear of a person's alter-ego travelling through space; it is the mind realising its freedom. For instance, Muhammad's astral journey from Mecca to Jerusalem may have been a similar experience. A telepathic journey often assumes that the mind embarks upon a project in which the physical body cannot share. In so-called telescopic experiences vivid scenes from the past appear before us and we are convinced that 'we have been there before'. Moreover, there is the kind of experience known as 'spirito-mental' which the 'free' mind knows but of which the time-bound mind is unaware. Or when men like St. Paul, or El Greco or Blake see visions which are too awful to describe, what has really happened? The mind has found a dimension of its own. In the vision a new truth may be revealed, or a neglected need brought to light, or a visitor from another world may appear. In any case, any communication in the spirito-mental dimension is quite independent of time, body or will.

When some of these gifts appear in the life of a person, we regard him as extraordinary. A person who has attained such extraordinary powers may also have the power to win a response from others. Moreover, faith and expectation are deepened when we are in the presence of such a person. If we are in the presence of the infinite and the inspired, will not our minds be attuned to the wonders that may occur in such an environment?

The following story of Narada shows how a young Hindu found liberation through meditation and constant seeking.[16] His mother went out of the house at night to milk the cow and was bitten by a cobra and died. 'I saw' he said, 'that even this event may serve my salvation'. His story is told in truly evangelical tones. 'I was lost in meditation with thoughts kindled by love, and with eyes filled with tears of longing. Then came the Lord, descending into my heart and I entered into his peace'. After this remarkable experience, here is the song which Narada sang:

He who coloured the swan white,
Who painted the parrot green,
Who created the peacock's splendour,
He will also care for me.
Whether I walk or stand, work or worship,
Whether I sing or eat or drink,
Constantly stands on the tip of my tongue,
That word, that only exalted name, O Narayana!

His belief in his Lord Narayana prompted his renunciation. His Lord became the abiding and unbroken element in his life. The same thought is expressed in the Gita: 'Man is created out of faith. As man believes, so he is'.

There is another story in the Vishnu Purana[17] about a king who became angry when he heard about his son, Prahlada's piety. He asked the boy's guru whence this odd concern with sacred things had come. The guru replied, 'Do not be angry with me, O King; your son has not got it from me'. The King then turned to his son:

Tell me quick, who taught you this?
Your teacher says it was not he.

Prahlada answered:

He Himself, the Teacher of the world,
He Vishnu, who dwells in our hearts.

To the one who seeks moksha through faithful seeking and continuous meditation, his teacher becomes Vishnu himself. Or, as the Friends of God claimed in Germany: 'We have but one teacher, the Spirit of God'.

Hindus believe that even in Moksha itself their souls will appear before Bhagavan to answer many questions. One of these will be: 'Why have you not come here long ago, my friend?' The soul answers, 'Because I had lost the connections with thee, while I, fool that I was, took the body to be 'I', not knowing that thou dwelt in me'. There is little doubt, therefore, that one of the ultimate benefits of meditation is salvation

itself. Whatever our religion, we are debtors to divine grace. Let
Narada speak for us all:

> *To serve him, that is peace.*
> *What want has he who has his grace?*
> *Away with pleasure and delight,*
> *Too small it is for him whose aim is high.*
> *One fruit alone can stay my sin,*
> *It is the fruit that is given to him,*
> *Who with steadfast mind has turned*
> *From the world of woes to the wonder-tree.*

The Way of Enlightenment or Samadhi

We have now considered succeeding phases of the meditation
process and now we come to the culmination. This end was in
view from the beginning and it is called samadhi or fulfilment.
There are still three hindrances which must be carefully overcome. The first hindrance is delusion. The inner being is sometimes deluded into thinking that inertia, lethargy and sleepiness
are some sort of substitute for detachment. Samadhi is not
passive resignation but active fulfilment. It may bring a feeling
of unease since the nearer we are to the goal, the deeper the
awareness of failure.

> *They who fain would serve thee best*
> *Are conscious most of wrong within.*[18]

It is a mistake to think of samadhi as a dreamy quietism, it is
rather a new sense of alertness and a keen sensitivity.

This keen sensitivity underlines the attachment to transient
things. It may be that this attachment has been present all
along but now it is regarded as a serious hindrance. How sad it
seems that even at this stage attachment to things is so pro-
nounced. Tagore is haunted by this thought:

> *But what of the evening time?*
> *When you find your boat sinking*
> *Within sight of the shore.*[19]

Restless emotions, human passions and the power of the senses still hold sway. Efforts must still be made to reach a state of 'uncolouredness', a state in which ideas and attitudes are not dominated by emotional responses. And even though human passions are not the threat that they were previously, they must be minimised even further by concentration on the attainment of samadhi. The senses, which once were so dangerous, have now become the servants of our highest aim. Each one now becomes an object of meditation. So hearing, touching, seeing, tasting and speaking intensify the bliss of samadhi. Attachment to anything other than Brahman is now seen as error. Also the reason for detachment is now understood. It involves unconcern since we are no longer concerned about consequences, it involves equanimity since we are no longer affected by ambition, and it involves transcendence since we are no longer in bondage to our surroundings.

The other hindrance is depression. This may be due to the failure to reach an ideal. Arjuna was anxious because he thought that he might fail to reach the ideal he sought. But Krishna allayed his anxiety by telling him that depression was the result of conflict between the roles of body, mind and spirit. He was assured that once he was clear about his role, the other anxieties would fade away.

We must now consider the different types of samadhi. In the first place, there are meditations on external objects and then on the mind itself. In meditating upon external objects we may take special notice of the size, shape, colour, intensity, nearness or distance of the object. However, the central purpose of meditation will be to discover something beyond the external object. To achieve this will be relatively easy, but meditation on the mind itself is much more difficult. Perhaps in prayer a man may say, 'Listen to me, I am thinking thy thoughts' and that is a good definition of prayer. But how often does he address his own mind with the words, 'As you think, I am listening to your thinking'. This is another way of saying that external objects are not needed when images and themes and visions arise in the mind. Yet the mind still expects more. Like the sages of old, he feels that:

Brighter visions beam afar.[20]

And even such holy aspirations betray the presence of desire. That is why this type of samadhi is called 'seed-bearing samadhi' because the seeds of desire and past action or karma have not been fully destroyed. A devotee may have samadhi without moksha.

There is another kind of samadhi which is attained by constant practice and this results in mental equanimity. The mind is trained to mark-time. It retains its present impressions but does not add to them. It therefore holds on to ideas, images and concepts which sustain goodness while refusing to allow anything else to enter. This method presupposes a very high system of control. This is known as a 'seed-holding samadhi'. Yet even this is not the ultimate goal. Unless the devotee achieves a complete lack of attachment even to this ideal, he is destined to become 'merged in nature' and may still be bound by karma. If in the first type of samadhi we may say that a devotee is still on the pilgrimage, in this second type we may say that he has reached the vestibule of moksha. He may even realise that his number of existences is limited. But only when he ceases to seek the highest will a devotee know that he has reached it. Then there will be no need to seek further. There is only one thing to know, that longing is at an end. He will not add to his adverse karma but neither will he add to his benign karma. This is what is meant by 'seed-holding samadhi'.

There are, however, some who reach the final goal. They succeed in abandoning all desire and all attachments and find the highest spiritual ecstasy. The absence of all such desires indicates the experience of moksha or liberation. The wisdom thus attained is shared only with the giver of it. The lake of the mind is now still, without a ripple or a wave. This is the culmination of life's pilgrimage. This is the 'seedless samadhi' from which no earthly existence may follow. The seeds which produce the karmic fruit no longer exist.

The question is sometimes asked as to whether samadhi experiences are compatible with a world-transforming activity. This is like asking whether saints are necessary. Anyone who attains any stage of samadhi represents a victory of the human spirit over environment, self and separateness. Each spiritual contribution of this sort is part of a world-transforming process.

References

1. Rabindranath Tagore, *Towards Universal Man*, (Intro-duction) Asia Publishing House.
2. Rabindranath Tagore, *Gitanjali* III, Macmillan
3. R. E. Hume (Trans.), *The Thirteen Principal Upanishads*, Mundaka III, Oxford
4. W. Wordsworth, *Longer Poems of William Wordsworth*, J. M. Dent
5. Rabindranath Tagore, *Gitanjali* XCIII & XCIV, Macmillan
6. S. Radhakrishnan, *An Idealist's View of Life*, Unwin, p. 121
7. F. E. Hutchinson (Ed.), *The Poems of George Herbert*, Oxford, p. 132
8. W. H. McNeill & Jean W. Sedlar (Ed.), *Classical India*, (The story is a free interpretation of two dialogues in the Brihadaranyaka and Chandogya Upanishads.) Oxford, pp. 188-196
9. A. A. Macdonell, *Hymns from the Rig-veda*, Rig-veda Book I
10. Anon, Poem: The Wayward Angel
11. R. W. Emerson, *The Works of Ralph Waldo Emerson*, Routledge, p. 1
12. Letter to the Romans XII.1
13. Juan Mascaró (Trans.), *The Bhagavad Gita*, Penguin, Book VI.11-14
14. Job XXXII.8
15. Juan Mascaró (Trans.), *The Bhagavad Gita*, Penguin, Book II.58
16. R. Otto, *Christianity and the Indian Religion of Grace*, Christian Literature Society, p. 34
17. Vishnu Purana, *Prahlada's Piety*
18. Methodist Hymn Book, 689.5
19. Rabindranath Tagore, *Three Plays*, Oxford, p. 35
20. Methodist Hymn Book, 119.3

The Buddhist Way

The Buddhist Way

Introduction

Gautama's Enlightenment

Eight Stages of the Holy Path:

1.	Correct understanding	— the nature of existence
2.	Correct aspiration	— the nature of the human search
3.	Correct speech	— the importance of communication
4.	Correct action	— the relation of karma to conduct
5.	Correct vocation	— the conditions of an ideal society
6.	Correct concentration	— the use of the will
7.	Correct meditation	— the awareness of mental and spiritual resources
8.	Correct attainment	— the blessings of Nirvava

Introduction

To stay on the Holy Path is the responsibility of the individual himself. It is not necessary to undertake careful preparation at this stage, he simply starts from where he is. It would not be necessary to stress this truth if it were generally recognised and acted upon. The trouble is that many believe that they must start from a different stance. This is partly the reason for the frantic unrest in human life, the conviction that they must begin from somewhere else. Moreover, an individual is not looking for truth in the general sense, he is looking for what is true for him. He may think that someone else has an advantage because he has a better starting-point, but this is because he is not prepared to face himself.

On this Path everyone is a pilgrim, and the problems and obstacles of one pilgrim will be different from those of another. But each pilgrim is on a journey from the known to the unknown, from the unreal to the real, from the transitory to the unchanging, from the desire for enlightenment to its re-alisation. To the Buddhist it is unthinkable that one life only should bring the individual to the desired goal. Like Bunyan's pilgrim he faces many hazards, obstacles, and temptations; unlike Bunyan's pilgrim there are no companions to encourage or discourage him in his enterprise. For this is a lonely road, a solitary experience in which self-discovery is the pilgrim's main concern. No saviour moves ahead of him through the valley, no gentle guide leads him to the delectable mountains, no faithful companion comforts him when he comes to the last river. He moves forward alone, facing each problem, making each decision, and accepting the consequences himself. All this is done in the certainty of only one thing: that there can be no certainty.

> *Therefore go forth companion; when you find*
> *No highway more, no track, all being blind,*
> *The way to go shall glimmer in the mind.*
> *Though you have conquered earth, and chartered sea,*
> *And planned the courses of all stars that be,*

Adventure on, for from the littlest clue
Has come whatever worth man ever knew.
The next to lighten all men may be you.[1]

The faint heart will ever seek some resting-place, some weak
finality, some present reassurance, but for the strong the word
is: 'walk on'. The great attainment is not to say 'I have arrived'
but 'I am becoming'. The traveller on the Path must always be
aware of certain dangers: for instance, imagining that he has
already attained, refusing to walk on, walking on without
realising that there is no certainty of reaching the goal.

One of the blessings of the Holy Path is the voluntary acceptance of the afflictions it may bring. Of course, it is possible to
choose an easier path and that is all very well so long as it is
realised that it is not the Path. It is easy to succumb to a temptation which has bedevilled religious history through the centuries,
the danger of adapting the Path to the peculiar needs of the
traveller. No doubt Gautama had learned from Vedanta philosophy that there are two tendencies in human nature: to manipu-
late the ideal so that it may be adapted to life itself; and secondly,
to elevate life to the ideal. The first of these is one of the great
temptations of our lives. If someone puts before us a certain
ideal and the first step towards reaching it is to give up self-
interest, self-enjoyment, and self-will, our immediate reaction
is to say that it is impracticable. What we really mean is that we
are not even prepared to consider whether it is a practical proposition or not. But if someone suggests an ideal which can
easily be reconciled with our selfishness, we accept it readily.
Yet it is the ideal that matters in the end. The belief that an
ideal is realisable makes it realisable. Although Jung's observation "what a man can be, he will be" is hard to verify histori-
cally, it honours human potentialities. The lower way is to
adapt and reduce the ideal to our poor endeavours, the higher
way is to raise our aims and aspirations to the level of the
ideal. In any case, the Path does not change so the hope that in
some way it may be adapted to man's needs is a forlorn one.
Kierkegaard refers to the same truth: "When a poor wayfarer,
whose feet are possibly sore, wincing at every step, almost drags

himself forward on the way, then there is much good sense in the thought of envying the rich who ride by him in comfortable carriages. For the highway is completely indifferent to the distinction of how one travels it, and it is undeniably pleasanter to drive in a comfortable carriage than to walk so oppressed. But in the spiritual sense that way is: how it is travelled; and then it would certainly be a strange thing if on the way of affliction there were some who walked without afflictions. The affliction is the way. If someone travels without afflictions, then so be it; then he merely goes on another road, which is his own affair. But doubt cannot lay hold on the sufferer and make him doubtful by the thought that others walk *on the same way* without afflictions".[2]

Still, the pilgrim is not without some encouragement. If he embarks on this journey of discovery and spiritual development, at least he knows that he is not a pioneer. Gautama trod this way to its destination. His was the supreme joy: he made the path as he travelled on it. Where one man has gone, others may follow, and the pilgrim may take comfort from this fact. But he must follow humbly and obediently if he is to reach the real destination. He should remember also that the path is not changed to suit him, but he must change in order to tread the path.

Moreover, treading the path requires the undivided faculties of the whole man. It is the attempt to compartmentalize human experience that often leads to fragmentation. The path must be trodden by the whole man and not merely by the intellect or the better self. Heart, mind, and will must develop equally. To depart from the path is its own punishment, for the steps must be retraced at whatever cost. There are no short-cuts and there can be no excuses. One of the characteristics of the law of karma is that it isolates the individual and holds him accountable for his actions. The path is a process of moral evolution according to the karmic law. Of course the pilgrim will profit from the courage and resolution of others, yet in no sense can their example be a substitute for his own effort. Still, their inspiration has a salutary effect. "When the Yogin sees that the hearts of others have been set free, he leaps forward by way of aspiration, to the various fruits of a holy life, and he makes efforts to attain the yet unattained, to find the yet unfound, to realize the yet unrealized."[3] It is a lonely journey, and since no individual is serving the same karma, it is an unprecedented journey too. Even Buddhas "do but point the way".

In Europe religion is understood as a sort of fixed relationship between the self and the Supernatural, the individual and the Absolute. East of Suez a spiritual relationship may only be described in terms of movement. It is a dynamic process, a travelling on a path. It is on this path that wisdom and compassion are to be found. Gautama himself was known as the Compassionate One and repeatedly he indicates that compassion is the paramount quality. He prevented war between rival communities; he returned to his father to explain the reasons for his renouncing the world; and overriding all was his concern that the whole creation should be released from suffering and sorrow. His enlightenment is described in metaphors taken from the created world: "A lotus, unspoiled by passion, sprung from the lake of knowledge; a cloud bearing the water of patience, pouring forth the Ambrosia of the good Law . . . causing all the shoots of healing to grow; a sun that destroys the darkness of delusion".[4] The impression is that nature herself somehow shares the new enlightenment.

Wisdom also is found on the path but not the wisdom that consists in answering every question or solving every problem; it is the wisdom gleaned whilst proceeding on the journey. This is what the Buddhist means when he says:

The Path exists but not the traveller on it.[5]

Gautama's Enlightenment

The moment we begin thinking about Buddhism we are inescapably plunged into a time-scale which is almost inconceivable in human terms. Buddhism does not begin with Siddhartha Gautama. But if we have to probe into aeons of time past to

trace his beginning, we have also to gaze into the distant future
to see his existence in its true dimension. Gautama, the Buddha,
belongs to cosmic and not merely to historical time. The eighty
years of his historical existence represent a mere speck in the
parabola of cosmic time. For thousands of years he was being
prepared in mind and spirit for the Buddhahood he was
confidently expected to attain. We contemplate with awe-struck
wonder his calm and patient endurance of the discipline and
suffering of many existences before the one that brought him
release and enlightenment.

Aeons before Gautama appeared, a young devotee named
Megha was informed by Lord Dipankara, himself a Buddha,
that he would one day attain that exalted spiritual state. So the
long pilgrimage began which was to culminate in the birth of a
prince of life and of death and of Nirvana. His coming marked
a new direction in the spiritual history of mankind.

Although born into a Hindu family his appearance did not
reaffirm the truths of Hinduism but rather moved away from
many of them into a new direction and a new way. It is now
generally recognised that Gautama was the latest avatar or
incarnation of Vishnu. We may, therefore, wonder why he
rejected some of the main tenets of Vaishnavite religion. We
may also be surprised that he introduced an entirely new system
of belief and conduct. This brings us to the Buddha's original
contribution to Indian thought, which, though revolutionary in
its consequences, was initiated by the least revolutionary of
men. He had no desire to break with his native religion but his
far-reaching ideas could not be contained within the Hinduism
he had inherited.

He never put forward a world view because he was not
greatly interested in this world. He never envisaged a perfect
social order because the social order itself was unreal. Since
the caste system was part of the social order, it too was a
massive illusion and need not, therefore, be taken seriously.
Already the axe was laid to the root of the tree, for the new
cult had undermined the long-standing prestige and influence
of the Brahmins who were responsible for perpetuating the
caste system. Still less was this new cult acceptable as it was

introduced by someone who was not a Brahmin. Gautama belonged to the Kshatriya caste and, therefore, could claim no
priestly lineage.

There was no doubt, however, that Gautama bore the marks
of a leader of strong individuality and power. Initially his was
the dynamism of purpose rather than action. Perhaps
unknowingly he had accumulated wisdom from previous existences, for he knew precisely what he wanted to do and why it
must be done. The discipline of such experiences had brought
him almost to the point of liberation, and he was determined
that nothing would hold him back now. Still, as of old, many
forces in the world were waiting to hold him in bondage. The
accepted stereotypes of society were unacceptable to him and
even his father's palace was a prison from which to escape. The
fact is that Gautama had now reached a stage when existence
itself was tortuous to bear. In some societies such a man would
have been regarded as an anti-social crank but by his early and
later disciples he became the herald, and his message the means,
of future liberation.

Gautama's persistent protests were disturbing and alarming
to the complacent society in which he was brought up. As much
by actions as by words he attacked the social and religious
structures of his age: the caste system, polytheism, idolatry,
priestly rule and hereditary religion. Even at an early age he
seemed to have sorted out and overcome his personal problems
and others were convinced that he had found a different wavelength from theirs. He had made the discovery that there was
one master-chain which held all other chains in place. He knew
that the bonds of Hinduism, of the past, of rebirths, of ignorance, of suffering, of transitoriness, and of change, would
remain intact until and unless the master-chain of self-centredness was broken.

At last there had appeared on the temporal scene a man
who saw the eternal dimension and who brought to bear on the
narrow prejudices of his time the thoughts of a cosmic mind.
In an acquisitive, hierarchical, and moribund society he firmly
proclaimed the self-renouncing way. His appeal was universal,
reasonable and logical, and for sheer logical consistency it is

still unsurpassed. He insisted on applying his own theories, and his experience of liberation became the central factor of his message.

The search for liberation was arduous and prolonged, for such an unparalleled blessing is never easily attained. He looked for an answer to the riddle of existence in the intricate speculations of the Hindu scriptures, but the answer was not there. He obeyed his advisers and studied the cumulative wisdom of the sages but the answer was not there. He tried the usual methods of asceticism: days of fasting, weary pilgrimages, deprivation of comforts, living in the jungle like a sannyasi, but the answer was not there. For a time this young prince even lived as an outcaste in the hope that the voluntary humiliation might bring liberation. But the answer was not there. None of these things affected his real condition, and the failure to find even the promise of enlightenment brought him to the nadir of despair. Their impact on his sensitive and innocent mind deepened his depression. Perhaps everything had forsaken him — gods, men, and animals. Perhaps even the idea of liberation was an illusion. No wonder such a sensitive and imaginative soul felt defeated and abandoned. Yet even the dark forebodings which were prompted by this futile search might be bearable if only they heralded the dawn of enlightenment. As for a Hindu lawyer of modern times, at the end of the searchings, the experiments and wistfulness, the crucial question remained:

> *Weary are we of empty creeds*
> *Of deafening calls to fruitless deeds;*
> *Weary of priests who cannot pray,*
> *Of guides who show no man the way:*
> *Weary of rites wise men condemn,*
> *Of worship linked with lust and shame;*
> *Weary of custom blind, enthroned,*
> *Of conscience trampled, of God disowned;*
> *Weary of men into sections cleft,*
> *And Hindu life of love bereft.*
> *Weary of life not understood,*
> *A battle, not a brotherhood;*

Weary of Kali Yuga years:
Frighted with chaos, darkness, fears;
Life is an ill, the sea of births is wide,
And we are weary; who shall be our guide?[6]

Gautama did not set out with the deliberate intention of rejecting the religion of his birth. Like many other reformers after him, he was no doubt surprised at his own discoveries and even more at their consequences. He asked questions and could not rest until some of them were answered. His discoveries were the outcome of his experience. He planned no attack on formal Hinduism and sought no quarrel with its exponents; he was carried along by the momentum of new truths. In Gautama's eyes these truths rendered many of the old ones obsolete. Of course it was one thing for him to think this but an entirely different thing to persuade others.

What then was the nature of this experience? Turning away from the speculative philosophy of the Upanishads, and from the severe ascetical practices recommended by the Jains, Gautama was at a loss to know what the next stop should be. One of the questions which haunted him was: why is there so much evil and suffering associated with human experience? The answer had not been revealed to him although he thought he had sought in the most likely and promising places. One evening he came to a quiet grove by a riverside and sat down to rest. He was low in spirit, feeling discredited and forsaken. It was a clear, still evening in the month of May, at the time known in India as cowdust, when the fierce heat of the day begins to fade and the gentle breeze brings some relief to the weary traveller. But for this traveller the weariness was physical only, his mind and spirit and emotions were waiting to receive. Truth came unbidden like the dawn, but it was not for him alone, but also for thousands of his followers who were to find the same light and follow the same path. He later told his friends: "Though skin, nerves and bone should waste away, and life-blood itself be dried up, here sit I till I reach enlightenment."

And e'er the westering sun went down,
Crowning that day with its crimson crown,
He knew that he had won.[7]

So there drew to a close one of those momentous days in the history of our race, a day whose influence does not diminish but rather grows even in an age of cynicism and despair. There broke forth from the lips of the seeker words which still stir deep chords within us and resound as one of the great triumphant songs of the ages:

Many a house of life
Hath held me — seeking ever him who wrought
The prison of the senses, sorrow frought;
Sore was my ceaseless strife!
But now,
Thou builder of this tabernacle — thou!
I know thee. Never shalt thou build again
These walls of pain,
Nor raise the roof tree of deceits, nor lay
Fresh rafters on the clay;
Broken thy house is, and the ridge-pole split:
Delusion fashioned it.
Safe pass I thence deliverance to obtain.[8]

In those moments the tyranny of the self was broken. The following sentence underlines the dramatic change that had taken place in Gautama's life. "This is my last existence, there will be no rebirth for me."

A sermon preached to King Bimbisara and his people gives the essence of the message that followed: "He who knows the nature of his self and understands how his senses act, finds no room for the 'I' and thus he will attain peace unending. The world holds the thought of 'I' and from this arises false apprehension. Ye that are slaves of the 'I', that toil in the service of self from morning to night, that live in constant fear of birth, old age, sickness and death, receive the good tidings that your cruel master exists not. Self is an error, an illusion, a dream. Open your eyes and awake. See things as they

are and you will be comforted. He who is awake will no longer
be afraid of nightmares. He who recognises the nature of the
rope that seemed to be a serpent ceases to tremble. He who has
found that there is no 'I' will let go all the lusts and desires of
egotism''. [9]

The Holy Path

The logic of the stages of the holy path is impressive. The way
in which each stage logically and consistently follows from the
preceding stage is sometimes overlooked. But if it is overlooked
the impact which Buddhism makes as a coherent philosophy of
life will be diminished. Let us underline this logical consistency
by giving a brief outline of the stages of the holy path. A
detailed analysis will follow.

1. The first task is to examine the nature of human existence.
We have to find out who and what we are. John Clare's line
summarizes the problem of the first stage:

I am: yet what I am none cares or knows[10]

Buddhism affirms that we have to find out. If there is something
wrong with our lives, what is it? If there is a serious dislocation
in the universe, what is it? If there is something wrong with our
understanding of the world, we must search it out.

2. If the first question is: how shall we understand ourselves in
relation to the world, the second question is: what do we really
want? Our present intellectual bewilderment and social chaos
may well have resulted from our refusal even to ask this
penetrating question.

3. However, our problem may be not so much that we have
been unaware of the question as that we have failed to articulate it. We have not formulated the question because we have
not recognised its immense significance. In fact our greatest
single asset — communication — has not only been under-used
but as far as this matter is concerned, unused.

4. It is because the lines of communication have broken down that we have not been aware of the practical action which may be taken to correct our ways. We cannot take appropriate action unless we have already defined what is needed. Action, however, must be taken positively and negatively if we are to reach our goal.

5. The action we take must be correct. That is to say it must be based on ethical principles. Far-reaching questions are involved therefore in this fifth stage: how should we spend our time? how far are we responsible for the welfare of others? how do we earn our living? what contribution do we make to the ideal society?

6. There must be the will to work for such a society. It will emerge only as a result of vision and imagination, energy and determination. It will require the maximum use of every faculty of every person if the desired end is to be attained.

7. Although each successive stage is important, it must be firmly understood that there cannot be a successful outcome unless there is an awareness of the spiritual resources which may be awakened and applied through meditation.

8. This is the way that will bring us to supreme bliss because it will lead us to unity with Absolute Reality. Whether we call it Nirvana or Kailas or T'ien or Heaven, it is immaterial, for it will be the end of suffering and change, of sorrow and strife, of separateness and self, and this is our true goal.

It is when we delineate the eight stages of the holy path in this way that we realise that Buddhism is accurately described as a philosophy of life. Now we must consider the first stage in greater detail. Correct knowledge means knowledge of the four holy truths of Buddhism. This amounts to a thorough investigation of the meaning and purpose of our existence. It is not merely a case of knowing these truths with our minds but of allowing them to work through our everyday concerns.

Intellectual knowledge is one thing, experiential knowledge is another. Truth is not only to be intellectually grasped, it must be lived through. It has to be proved by the individual in the depth of his being. It is even better when we realise that finding the true way is part of our destiny. But how shall we know that we are on the wrong track unless we cultivate self-observation? The equilibrium that we seek eludes us. Our attempts to root out evil desires are too weak and sporadic. Our will seems broken-backed and cannot help us; we seem prone to self-destruction. Thoughts that may destroy us are complacently harboured in our minds. Such thoughts are often the result of jealousy and resentment, fear and failure, and when they are given freedom of manoeuvre they infiltrate into our consciousness and take possession.

We suffer also from another serious disadvantage: so thoroughly and meticulously do we follow our habitual pattern in our thinking that we have no idea what is happening to us. For instance, we ask ourselves what is conventional, customary and advantageous, and without further ado, accept it. Yet the simple acceptance of this procedure is as injurious as deep prejudice or evil desire. It is not that we have given approval to these questionable tendencies, it is much more serious, for we have not even realised that they needed approval. This means that self-knowledge has been by-passed probably because it is not easily attained. Nevertheless, it is essential if the process which may end in self-destruction is to be halted. If it is not, we shall continue to act habitually, thoughtlessly and mechanically.

Even though some esoteric schools of Buddhism tend to transcend the functions of the mind and to aim at stages of awareness where the mind plays a minimal part, there is no doubt that Buddhism begins with a critical examination of things as they are. There may be room at later stages of development for belief, assumption, emotion and imagination, but at the beginning there is room only for observable facts. An assessment, even a confrontation of the world, precedes any idea of renunciation. Man is rational and needs to explore the world in which he lives. This exploration helps him to understand himself. Just as the elephant tests the track to see whether

it will bear his weight, so man treads warily, endeavouring to
discover whether he may proceed confidently and trustfully in
his environment. In other words he asks the question which
philosophers have asked across the centuries: is the world
amenable to reason? Any discoveries that are made are promptly
subjected to reason. The situation is a complex one because
man, as the custodian of reason, is his own arbiter. But reason
is engaged in a dialogue and not a monologue. Man conducts a
continuous dialogue with the world and with his own self. His
future and his present ultimately depend upon the outcome of
this dialogue. Sometimes reason addresses self, which often
represents involuntary intuitions, with the words: "I don't
believe that and you are not going to believe it either". At
other times, however, these intuitions will be readily approved
by reason. Let us suppose that the dialogue is something like
this: Self: 'Everywhere I look I see signs of suffering'. Reason:
'I agree'. Self: 'But I can't bring myself to believe that this is
how things were meant to be'. Reason: 'No matter, this is how
things are'. Self: 'I believe that somewhere the explanation of
these things is known and I will rest content with that'. Reason:
'If there is an explanation, you must find it'. Now the great
merit of Buddhism is that intuition accepted reason's challenge.
This acceptance involved a penetrating examination of the
meaning of human existence.

The Buddha affirmed that the main characteristics of
human existence are dukkha — suffering, anicca — transciency,
and anatta — fragmentation or non-self. Suffering implies
mental and physical ill. It includes moral evil as well, although
this is not sufficiently recognised in Buddhist teaching as a
whole. If Gautama had stopped at this first characteristic —
the universality of suffering — he would surely have become
demoralized. This would also be true of the human race as a
whole, for unrelieved suffering without any known reason or
explanation would imply permanent despair and the extinction
of hope. Even though further questions must be asked which
may or may not alleviate the situation, the prevalence of suffering is undeniable. It is possible to engage in a sort of cover-up
using superficial rationalizations. One example is to say that

suffering is fortuitous or vicarious or inevitable, but this merely underlines the problem without explaining it. It has to be admitted that the human pilgrimage is marked by tragedy. Birth involves suffering, so does decay, sickness and death. To have to endure what is disliked involves suffering, to be separated from what we love and respect means suffering, and to be denied personal fulfilment and satisfaction brings suffering. But why emphasize a fact so unpalatable? It is precisely because it is unpalatable that we have built our facades pretending that the truth is not what we know it to be.

The admission of such truth is sometimes regarded as unrelieved pessimism. But if pessimism is one of the chief characteristics of our human predicament, it is a gain, not a loss, to acknowledge it. Therefore, Buddhism affirms that human existence is inseparable from suffering. This suffering is physical, mental and spiritual, and unless a cure or an explanation is found, it will result in disillusionment and despair.

> *Man this heavy load must bear,*
> *The laying down thereof is bliss.*

Dukkha is the result of too strong an attachment to present existence — samsara. Folly is added to the pain because attachment to samsara means attachment to what is impermanent. How did Gautama reach the stage of detachment? Three 'passing sights' radically changed his attitude. He saw a person suffering from an incurable disease, another physically crippled with age, and a corpse being carried to the riverside. Appalled by what he saw he was determined no longer to cling to an existence which was painful and transient. The fourth 'passing sight' convinced him in his resolution. A man of serene countenance, with a slow measured tread and simple attire, came walking by. He had the look of one who had renounced the material world and overcome sensual desires. This was a holy man. Gautama knew that this man held the secret that all must strive to know.

Life involves suffering and transiency, it is also characterised by fragmentation or egolessness — anatta. This means that there is no such thing as self in the sense of an individual unit. There is merely an assemblage of five separate elements or skandhas as they are called. These skandhas which we imagine constitute a unified sentient being are matter, feelings, perceptions, acts of will, and consciousness. We are under the impression that because these elements function simultaneously in one human life they form a separate self. That is part of our illusion. The five elements themselves are separate and transient so how can they constitute a permanent reality?

We must now turn to the second stage of the holy path. What is involved in the phrase "Correct aspiration"? The important question is: "What do we really want?" If we can find an answer to this question, we can find an answer to another which is related to it: how may we obtain what we really want? It is one of the maladies of our race that when it is most sure of what it wants, it generally wants the wrong things. Or to put it more accurately, it does not want the things that are beneficial and of permanent value. Man is not usually aware of these forces which take control of his aspirations and sometimes he does not perceive the difference between genuine and false aspirations. The plea of Mephistopheles to gain control of the mind of Dr Faust still sounds plausible enough:

> *There's still a chance to gain him,*
> *If unto me full leave you give*
> *Gently upon my road to train him.*

Before very long, in spite of Faust's noble intentions and high-flown ambitions, his fate was summed up in a single line:

> *Thirsting for truth, went wretchedly to error*[11]

Faust's predicament is a common one. It is not that man has no ambition or driving force, it is that he often begins from a false motivation. He is full of aspirations but they are so self-centred that they bring only sorrow and disillusionment in their train.

There was a man of Ch'i who desired to have gold. One fine day he went out early in the morning to market. He went straight to the gold dealer's shop, snatched the gold away and walked off. When the officers arrested him they questioned him: 'Why, the people were all there; why did you take the gold in broad daylight?' And the man replied, 'I didn't see any people, I saw only the gold'.[12] Perhaps man never sees beyond his own needs. Perhaps he does not wish to see beyond his needs. If he goes through life grasping and plundering and hoarding, what will the consequences be? Not only will he hurt others in his fierce ambition but he will be hurt himself. If this is his plight he will be lost in a circle of self-centredness. Perhaps the best thing man can do is to make a careful analysis of his predicament so that a way forward can be found. But this is not new; the question was asked and answered by Matthew Arnold:

> *What is the course of the life of mortal men on earth?*
> *Most men eddy about here and there — eat and drink,*
> *Chatter and love and hate, gather and squander, . . .*
> *Striving blindly, achieving nothing.*[13]

Buddhism asked the same question and gave a similar answer long ago. Man is lost in a multiplicity of things and he has little hope of reaching his true goal until and unless he becomes aware of his condition. He must have room to be and to grow. It is well known that every plant must have room to breathe and grow, to receive sunlight and rain, and to be free from being choked by weeds or retarded by too much shade. Human life also requires freedom, freedom to be, to aspire, and to serve. It is easy to cry 'Peace, peace' when there is no peace. Or to cry 'Freedom, freedom' when there is no freedom. In matters of individual action freedom is impeded by misdirected emotional drives, psychological blocks, unresolved inhibitions, and personal idiosyncracies. Such problems cannot be resolved in the twinkling of an eye. They may not even be recognised as problems at all. But it is essential that they should be recognised and analysed and understood. Unless this is done, everything will be clouded by self-deception, and aspiration will be nullified.

To say that Buddhism can be summed up as 'the modifying of obstacles' may be an over-simplification, nevertheless it is a very strong element in this second stage of the holy path. Whatever prevents free and clear thought, free and clear aspiration, is an obstacle. It is precisely in this area that Buddhism is sometimes misrepresented. If everything is unreal, impermanent, and characterised by ill, why should anyone be concerned about life at all? If there was nothing more to say than this, pessimism would overwhelm us all. However, if we are aware of our predicament, we may be spurred on to seek the real, the permanent, and the good. Buddhism is emphatic that there is an existence that is real, permanent, and blissful. But where? And how is it to be attained? Again we are driven back to the question of correct aspiration or to use a more familiar word — motivation.

Motivation implies individual choice. The holy path has two directions lest the elements of choice be treated too lightly: the right hand way leads through benevolence to the welfare of humanity, the left hand way leads through selfishness to spiritual death. If the removing of obstacles indicates the negative side, what constitutes the positive side? "The Path is viewed from two angles: the one is experienced as 'obstacle removing', the other as the feeling of 'being freed' from what was formerly disturbing and obstructing. Gradually this will lead to a state in which the aspirant has no longer to learn".[14a] Having learned the important lessons for himself and having no further anxiety about his spiritual development, he will be free to offer himself in love and service to others. He cannot, however, offer what he does not possess, and his altruism will be limited unless he is committed to the attaining of his goal. Guenther emphasizes this truth: "As an index of man's spiritual growth and his experience of it, the path is intentional in structure. That is to say, I cannot go without going somewhere; I cannot think without thinking about something; and I cannot do without doing something . . . This means that the objective is a challenge to make up one's mind about it and to take a stand. In grasping or accepting these possibilities man has already made up his mind about what he is seeking, and in following the path he discards whatever may prevent him from attaining his goal".[14b]

Martin Buber who readily acknowledged the influence of Buddhism upon his own thought, suggests three types of persons and the one that he warmly commends comes nearest to the man who is at the second stage of the holy path. The three types are as follows: there is the person who has no wish to give himself to the other in any circumstances. He is the non-partner. His background may in some way prevent him from real participation. There is, of course, a difference between the person who has no wish to participate and one who is psychologically incapable of doing so. The second type of person is the 'seeming' man. He is concerned with what others think of him. He tries to make himself appear spontaneous and sincere or whatever he thinks will win the approval of the other. But this pretence destroys the authenticity of life between persons. The third type is the one who gives himself spontaneously without thinking of the image he awakens in the beholder. This man acts in his true being. He gives himself completely.[15] This is precisely the position of the aspirant at the second stage of the holy path.

This type of aspirant is 'other-directed'. He is not 'tradition-centred' for that would be associated with unreformed Hinduism which Gautama had rejected. Nor is he 'inner-directed' for that would involve direct access to God which is not envisaged in Buddhism. It is interesting to note that a western sociologist rejects the state of other-direction for two reasons. First, because it encourages feelings of individual insignificance, and second, because it reflects an impoverishment of the personality. For the very same reasons the other-directed aspirant is warmly commended in Buddhist teaching.

The other-directed individual subordinates his own values to the expectations of other people who surround him. Universal benevolence which is a significant phrase in Buddhism begins here. At first sight, the phrase seems to be too general and nebulous to be practicable. But universal benevolence is simply the cumulative result of individual choices and attitudes.

In everyday affairs and actions the ultimate concern is the welfare of others, and even though the effects of this on the character of the person performing the actions may be incidental, it is unmistakable. In other words, the attitude of universal benevolence produces a benevolent person. The side-effects of this attitude are present even when they are not sought.

In any great enterprise the temptation is to grow weary in well-doing, to start well but soon to tire, to begin with bright dreams but soon to make excuses for their non-fulfilment. But if the aspirant has made his choice, and if he has recognised and removed the obstacles, and if he is resolved at all costs to reach the goal, he will not lose his vision nor turn back from his quest. He will discover that the way of selfless service is the way to the goal he seeks.

A Brahmin came to the Buddha bearing gifts in each hand. The Buddha said, 'Drop it'. The Brahmin let fall one of his gifts. Again the order came, 'Drop it'. The Brahmin dropped the other gift. Yet again the command came, 'Drop it'. He was puzzled this time but not too puzzled to smile as he realised that the light had come. For when he had nothing else to give, he could only give himself in selfless and ceaseless service for mankind.[16]

The third stage in the holy path is correct communication. The person who placed a portrait of Michelangelo opposite a modern abstract painting knew what he was doing. For whether the quizzical look on the face of the great artist is really there or only in the imagination of the onlooker is really immaterial, the meaning is clear. The lines of communication between one century and another are difficult to maintain. The problem, however, is much wider than this. It may be due to differences of language and culture, of class and ideology, or it may be due to the different outlook and values between one generation and another.

The Buddha showed remarkable insight in pin-pointing this matter of correct communication. When communications fail, the consequences for mankind are usually far-reaching. It is sad to relate that when the technical facilities for communication are far advanced, real communication has not been achieved. Anyone who has heard the fateful words: "We have not received an answer to our ultimatum", knows that from that moment uncontrollable forces are unleashed. Why? One nation ceases to talk to another, no one knows what to say. The end of communication spells death. This is one reason why this stage of the holy path is so important. It will not do to dismiss the matter by saying that its meaning is self-evident. The fact is that some failures of communication affect everyone.

No doubt the Buddha was thinking mainly of speech as a medium of communication. Speech may be incorrect. It may mean monologue rather than dialogue, it may convey ill-considered notions, dogmatic assertions, trivial observations and malicious ideas. All these are forms of communication but undesirable forms. Speech is not now the only medium of communication. We must now include radio and television programmes, advertising material, newspapers, magazines and books. The process of correction is not an easy one. What we see as well as what we hear, what we think as well as what we speak, require the refining process.

Certainly communication is important, but communication of what? It must be the communication of truth. Untruth diminishes one's being, deceives the one who is addressed and increases his difficulties when truth is offered. There must be certain rules if correct communication is to be possible. For instance, words must carry the meaning usually attributed to them and they must be used with precision. This is what Eliot meant when he wrote:

> *And every phrase*
> *And sentence that is right (where every word is at home,*
> *Taking its place to support the others,*
> *The word neither diffident nor ostentatious,*
> *An easy commerce of the old and the new,*
> *The common word exact without vulgarity,*
> *The formal word precise but not pedantic,*
> *The complete consort dancing together)*
> *Every phrase and every sentence is an end and a beginning,*
> *Every poem an epitaph.*[17]

When this happens, words will be vehicles of communication. Through words we learn something about the background, culture and activities of an individual. But most of all, we learn something about him, his character, aspirations and sensibilities.

Now this does not mean that every sincere statement is automatically regarded as truth. Nor does it mean that fact and truth are invariably the same. But it does mean asking ourselves the plain question: how many times do we deviate from the truth and why? This does not simply mean resolving to stop uncharitable speech but questioning the motive behind all speech. It is not enough to say, 'I must not say that because it is unfair or dangerous or cruel', we must recognise that wrong speech diminishes our own being.

The significance of this is often under-estimated. Speech is the vital link between two individuals. It may not always result in good relationships but it produces real relationships. There is no real relationship unless something passes between two persons, and this fact gives a deeper dimension to the whole question of speech. "Right speech as taught by the Enlightened One is comprehended in four distinct prescriptions: that men should speak only that which is true, that they should not speak what is false; that they should not speak evil of others, that they should refrain from slander; that they should not use angry and abusive language towards any fellow man, that they should speak kindly and courteously to all; and finally, that they should not indulge in pointless, foolish talk but let their speech be sensible and to the purpose".[18]

If truth is spoken to us, do we hear it and receive it as truth? Communication means really listening as well as truthfully speaking. The trouble is that we learn one side of the process but not the other. For most of the time we have turned off the receivers either because we don't want to listen, or we don't know how to listen, or we don't believe that what is being said is significant for us. Sometimes we are so preoccupied listening to ourselves that we have no time to listen to others. Sometimes we hear a noise without hearing words, and even when we hear words they are not always understood. For words become impoverished and do not convey the meaning intended.

If we are concerned about what we hear, we shall need a greater alertness and awareness. If we are intent on seeking truth, we shall listen. In seeking to discover truth we shall ask ourselves what our own discoveries of truth mean to us. If they mean something to us, we shall listen with genuine attention, for listening is an important part of communication. Few people have expounded this concept more clearly than Buber: "Sometimes we feel an urge to thank our fellow man even if he has not done anything special for us. For what then? For really meeting me when we met; for opening his eyes and not mistaking me for someone else; for opening his ears and listening carefully to what I had to say to him, indeed for opening up to me what I really wanted to address — his securely locked heart".[19] This depicts the essence of real communication. Really meeting, really seeing, really listening, and really giving one's full attention, amounts to a way of behaving. This way of behaving is presupposed in the third stage of the holy path. Communication, therefore, is a way of knowing other people and recognising them for their true worth, and of knowing ourselves, who and what we are. Behaviour is the way in which one person relates to another. The same principle applies to communities as well as individuals. When these ideas are collated, a code of conduct is the outcome and this code is plainly stated by the Buddha: "He avoids lying. He speaks the truth. Wherever he may be he never knowingly speaks a lie, either for the sake of his own advantage, or for the sake of any advantage whatsoever. He avoids tale bearing. What he has heard here, he does not repeat there; and what he has heard there, he does not repeat here, so as to cause dissension here. Thus he unites those that are divided; and those that are united, he encourages. Concord gladdens him, he delights and rejoices in concord; and it is concord that he spreads by his words."[20]

In considering the fourth stage of the holy path we must recall Gautama's debt to the Hindu faith in which he was brought up. Almost all religions teach a doctrine of redemption but they differ as to its meaning and ultimate form. Redemption in Hindu thinking is the desire for deliverance from the seen and the temporal. The material world of seen and temporal things is regarded as wholly evil, and the true and holy man is he who gets away from the bondage of the material world.

From this desire come the doctrines of karma and transmigration. Karma means action and this is the key word in

this fourth stage. Human deeds are either good or evil. No deed
can be neutral in its effects. Action determines the life and
status of the individual, and if in the course of one life an individual is not able to be purged from the contamination of the
material world, his actions will necessitate his rebirth until he
wins release. Redemption for the Hindu means release from this
bondage to rebirths.

In the search for enlightenment Gautama accepted the
Hindu interpretation of redemption. We must, therefore,
consider the merits and demerits of the doctrine as a whole.
Life in quality and quantity is accurately meted out and is the
fitting expiation of actions done in a previous existence. This
process continues until knowledge breaks through and breaks
up the seed of actions thus making transmigration impossible.
Those who do not attain this knowledge are brought back to
this world, but those who attain it find unity with Brahman.

The karma theory has its merits. It postulates a moral law
of cause and effect which is absolutely binding. Each action has
its reaction on life. This suggests an answer to the problem of
suffering. Suffering is the result of actions committed in a
previous existence. Karma offers, therefore, a plausible reconciliation between the facts of life and the claims of abstract
justice. But karma does more than this: it points to the necessity
of expiation. If it is true that whatever a man sows, he reaps,
then the reaping in itself is a form of expiation. Just because no
one can escape karma, not only is justice done to the moral
sense but the hope of ultimate release is kept alive. Forgiveness
and release cannot be obtained without cost and continuous
struggle. Evil brings bondage and is itself bondage. But we must
not forget that karma fosters the hope of complete release
eventually.

> *When are liberated all*
> *The desires that lodge in one's heart,*
> *Then a mortal becomes immortal;*
> *Therein he reaches Brahman.*[21]

Karma also does something to explain the inequalities of
man's lot in life. When suddenly calamity strikes a man's life, it

is natural to ask for an explanation. Of course, it may be answered that there is no explanation, but that indicates a more fatalistic despair than is envisaged in the karma theory. Job was trying to answer a similar question. The book was written to show the inadequacy of the theory that the good prosper and only the evil are unfortunate. But in the end Job has to fall back on God's inscrutable wisdom while at the same time not overlooking man's inscrutable waywardness. Job's friends, however, referred to sins committed in this life, so he was able to rebut them. Since the Hindu, like the rest of us, has no knowledge of his previous existence, he is less sure that his suffering is undeserved.

Even so the principle of retribution is a powerful factor in the karma theory. What we sow we reap implies a connection between sin and suffering.

> *Who plants mangoes, mangoes shall he eat;*
> *Who plants thorn-bushes, thorns shall wound his feet.*[22]

However, it is one thing to recognise the reality of retribution, but another thing to treat it as a final principle. It is easy to say "Good deeds produce happiness and bad deeds produce sorrow", but who would wish to be treated in terms of exact balance? In any case, punishment, to be just, should concern not deeds but their doer. It is not much help to a man if he carries over his sin from a past existence, but not the wisdom and experience to be gleaned from his errors. Still karma applies to all, and to this extent justice is implicit in it. This inspires resignation in some and serenity in others, but they may have to wait a long, long time before deliverance is possible.

Although karma offers an apparently simple and ready answer to the problem of evil, is it a satisfactory answer? One of the difficulties is that it postulates a negative theory of redemption. Aversion towards death is turned into an aversion towards life, and release from rebirth implies the spurning of all contact with the world. Not only does the theory undervalue any good that is in the world, it renders it devoid of any value at all even to the point of unreality. The believer in karma tends to remember the past, reject the world, and fear the future. It offers little comfort and joy, and although there is an element of hope, its long-term nature is such as to diminish any immediate motivation.

There is another serious defect: karma assumes that the consequences of evil are finite. But if they are regarded as finite, man himself can expiate them. If they are infinite, only God can expiate them. If God does this, it is reasonable to suppose that he will do it once-for-all. Such an act would be of cosmic significance. Perhaps, in the end, only the offer of forgiveness can break the bondage of the past.

Does karma stand the test of experience? The great advances made by the Dravidians in the areas of literacy, general education and social improvements, appear to negate the basic assumption of karma. For if all things are predetermined by an inexorable past, how can the improvements in their present condition be accounted for? Certainly many things were against the Dravidians — colour, heredity, educational disadvantages and social neglect. Many factors have contributed to this situation: lack of leadership, economics, the caste system, and the absence of adequate representation in government. When these reasons are given, the old belief in a fortuitous and unpredictable karma tends to diminish. So many people today are not prepared to accept the fatalism that karma implies. They believe that man has at least some say in his destiny. He is not at the mercy of inexorable fate. If he wills, he can change his life-style. New opportunities, new personal responses and the spread of literacy have weakened the karmic stranglehold.

Even so the karma theory achieves two important purposes: it keeps alive hopes of a better future in another existence and it motivates sound morality in the present. Since everyone hopes for a better future, everyone endeavours to perform those actions which will lead to beneficial results. It will be seen, therefore, that correct action is a concept borrowed by Gautama from his native Hinduism and incorporated as an important stage in the holy path.

Correct means of livelihood

In considering the fifth stage of the holy path it is necessary to reflect on the five precepts which have played an important part in Buddhist teaching.

The five precepts are:

1. To refrain from taking life and from harming any living thing.
2. To refrain from taking what is not given.
3. To refrain from the misuse of the senses.
4. To refrain from false speech.
5. To refrain from drugs and intoxicants which tend to cloud the mind.

Some of these precepts are self-evident and need little elaboration. But one glance at them is sufficient to indicate that if they were successfully carried out, an extensive social and moral revolution would follow. Indeed, their implementation would revolutionise modern society. Of course it is easy to give lip-service to such precepts but Gautama wanted something more than that. He insisted on the resolute intention to translate these precepts into the transactions of everyday life. They are so idealistic that often they are dismissed with a patronising nod of formal approval. Unfortunately this attitude has placed them in the category of unreachable ideals, and then, like everything else that is categorised, they are politely ignored. What happens when they are taken seriously?

Gautama was seeking to produce a society in which people would do nothing to damage their own lives or the lives of their fellow men, and would do everything to promote life rather than destroy it. If a man believes in the sanctity of life, there are some things that he is forbidden to do. Self-discipline imposes its own restrictions. He will not take that which is not given, and this refers to rape and adultery as well as to the more usual interpretations of theft. Yet it is not just a matter of his actions; his disposition will determine his actions. The key word here is 'respect', for if a man respects others, he will have no wish to harm them or steal from them or humiliate them. In other words he will have to examine all his attitudes and relationships to find out whether his contribution to society in terms of his profession and recreation is positive or negative, constructive or destructive. Some professions as well as some recreations will be closed to him. For instance, service in the Armed Forces or in an Arms Factory will be forbidden to him as will the slaughter of animals whether this is involved in his professional or leisure pursuits. Matters which previously have been dealt with in a casual and superficial manner will now be subjected to the most careful scrutiny by mind and conscience. Ethical questions will become more important to him than utilitarian considerations. The activating of conscience, mind, and sensitivity in dealing with practical matters will hopefully bring about changes in society. A more humane and compassionate society will replace the acquisitive and aggressive pattern.

Respect for life involves respect for all living creatures. "The law is plain, that life is sacred, be it that of a butterfly or a man. Let each then cultivate within his heart a genuine compassion for all forms of life, based on a reverence for its source and the oneness which such source entails, and commonsense decisions will be made in every case in which decision as to its application must be made".[23]

The last precept is a late addition but it needs to be re-emphasised in modern times. The aim of Buddhism is to attain mental, moral and physical control, and anything that detracts from this aim whether hard drugs or alcohol should be discouraged. This stage of the holy path may be summarised in the following words: "The path requires us to stop and consider how and why we are spending our working hours. It requires us to take time to think out and find some means of occupation which will be conducive to our own growth and development and which will, if possible, be beneficial to others. If a job helps us in our search for an understanding both of ourselves and of the world around us then it is, for us, samma ajiva —"no matter how futile and crazy it may seem to our friends and neighbours".[24]

We now come to the sixth stage of the holy path and this concerns correct effort. Effort is needed in developing insight, intuition and will power. This stage of the path deals exclusively with the thorough preparation that is needed in order to develop meditation techniques. Concentration is the key.

The meaning of bare awareness

In general the purposes of meditation are to know what is going on around us, beyond us and within us; to quieten the uproar, to diminish fantasy, and to find liberation from the ego-clutch. The Buddhist distinguishes between the kind of attention to things, persons and events which is accompanied by thinking, evaluating, assessing and relating, and the kind of attention which is altogether free from thought. The latter is 'bare' attention. It is an advanced form of concentration in which attention is not disturbed by noise, senses, or other distractions.

There is a difference between doing something and being aware that we are doing it. We can listen and be aware of ourselves listening. We can be aware of ourselves reading without ceasing to read. The first order of awareness is 'bare' attention, and the second order is conscious action. The monk who walks down the meditation hall with slow and measured tread is not day-dreaming. Far from it, he is keenly conscious of every step. What is going on within is reflected in what is going on outside. Inward calm is revealed in outward deliberation. So meditation first requires the cultivation of both orders of awareness.

How can this awareness be deepened?

Silence is both the preparation for and the result of profound awareness. Even though visual and audible aids have an important place in meditation, they are all dependent on the attainment of silence. Mandalas, mantras, and koans have their rightful place but a true understanding of their significance requires training in the uses of silence. "It is well said in Japan that any clown can tell the difference between wise talk and foolish talk, but it takes a good master to distinguish between wise silence and foolish silence".[25]

It is strange that silence is frequently equated with emptiness, as if it has no positive content. Silence evokes a deep consciousness which helps us to recognise and reject the artificial and superficial, and to take a serious look at things as they are. Tagore believes that for most of us life is no more than a meaningless game, and there is pathos and wistfulness in his comment:

> *They build their houses with sand,*
> *And they play with empty shells.*[26]

Silent waiting restores the balance to our lives for it produces a sense of expectancy. In such moments the inward eye is opened and new perspectives come into view.

> *From dawn till dusk I sit here before my door,*
> *And I know that of a sudden the happy moment will arrive*
> *When I shall see.*[27]

Moreover, it is a mistake to equate silence with inactivity. The building of Solomon's temple was a silent operation but doubtless the work was going on continuously and effectively.

> *No hammer fell, no ponderous axe was swung,*
> *Like some tall palm the noiseless fabric sprung.*

Yet so often it is assumed that silence means inactivity, and that nothing of importance happens without fuss and uproar.

The rewards of silence do not come by accident, it must be a chosen silence, a deliberate choice. It is good to use the casual and unsought opportunity when it comes but such an attitude makes no demands upon the will. Chosen silence often implies chosen solitude. We choose solitude but loneliness is imposed upon us and generally it is unwanted. Avoiding silence is tantamount to running away from ourselves, and most of our time is spent in this activity. We will do anything, go anywhere, serve anyone rather than give ourselves room to be. But this is what we need — room to be. It is in this sense that silence serves our existence. It is the debt we owe to our souls.

We listen often enough to the phoney self. We know his ploys and even know what he is going to say but have no power to stop him. When the real self says: "That's phoney and I'm not going to accept it", the phoney self knows that the real self is getting the measure of him. Frequently the phoney self wins because we cannot distinguish between the two voices. Only disciplined silence will produce this gift.

One of the reasons why it is desirable to seek silent solitude is because people and things and tasks are often no more than excuses and self-defences against being thrown back upon ourselves. We hide behind our duty and take shelter in our virtuous service. We may not be afraid of ourselves but we are afraid of what we might discover in the silent experience. The inward journey can no longer be avoided. Hugh St Victor had much in common with Buddhism when he said, "The way to ascend to God is to descend into oneself".

This chosen and disciplined silence must be a 'filled' silence too. This means that silence has its own contribution, a value of its own. We are obsessed with words and imagine that only words achieve anything worthwhile. There is such a thing as active silence. The content of silence may be a presence, a vision, a disclosure, even a revelation. Its language is felt not heard, experienced not analysed. It may bring us to the central reality — the "still point of the turning world" or to the still-centre in God. Some practical steps may be taken to achieve this experience. We can record the obstacles to silence for these will differ from one individual to another. We can learn the art of interpreting silence. Words are not the only vehicle of communication, and in any case words are sometimes made incomprehensible so that we have to learn what is being disclosed in other ways, perhaps in a new dimension of experience. The levels of human experience may be deepened when we allow this other medium to do its work. It is in this sense that silence serves our existence. Without this there is a whole area of experience that is never realised.

Silence should not be confused with neutrality as if all emotions and expectations were temporarily suspended. Silence may intensify such emotions and expectations. Nor should it be thought that silence will always bring pleasantness and serenity. "We may experience it as threatening, hostile, even as killing. We may experience it as boredom, tension, loneliness, insignificance, a state of being unloved, and as loss of identity. This dark face of silence is painful to look upon, and we long to be let off the encounter".[28] But silence must be faced even with its accompanying trials and pains. For we seek a silence which is not just emptiness or inactivity or neutrality but one which has its own content and achieves its distinctive purpose.

By understanding the value and uses of silence we shall be able to identify the cause of the uproar. Our task is to cultivate a clear, non-interfering awareness of what is going on. The more we practise this, the more we realise that what is happening in us is inseparably linked with what is happening outside us. Our contemplation and the responses and decisions which result from it, determine the world in which we live. If our responses are so important, they should be moulded in contemplation. The more we cultivate awareness, the richer and more satisfying our responses will be. Everything depends upon the measure of our response, but a complete response will not be possible if there is uproar within. When we stop, give attention, and look within, the initial impression is one of silent uproar. Silent because others are not aware of it, uproar because to us it sounds like thunder. Only meditation reveals how unbearable this uproar can be, it is strident, persistent and penetrating. Meditation accentuates it to identify and remove it. But it must be faced before it can be cured. We have a serious problem but we have become immune and our immunity is our malady. It has become a distraction from the real problem. We have lived with the uproar so long that we prefer to accommodate it rather than correct it. We only learn to live with this disability because we have not allowed meditation to reveal the condition. Unless we do this, we shall not be aware of the storm outside because of the noise of the thunder inside. It is essential that we trace the causes of the uproar.

There are noises caused by normal physiological processes such as twitches, aches, itches, sneezing, loud breathing, coughing and belching. In addition to these there is the continuous monologue of thought, imagery, and imagined speech which constantly stirs up feelings of resentment, bitterness and revenge. Then there is the ghostly background of half-formed mental activity, largely unconnected with any kind of emotional arousal. Along with these half-formed thoughts there are uncontrolled desires, broken promises and selfish impulses. There are also excuses, denials, self-defence and self-assertion. These become more active as we resist the need for solitude, silence and contemplation. The usual argument runs as follows: we haven't time to cultivate meditation, or we are not temperamentally suited to the practice. In any case the conditions of modern life don't allow for such eccentric exercises.

Even if success is achieved in dealing with those problems, the ego-clutch remains. The ego is preoccupied with holding on to the things it likes and the fading out of those it rejects. But this automatic switching off of the unpleasant is no answer to the problem. The ego has an obsessive need to compare itself with others all the time. Its roots are in fantasy — the fantasy that it is separate and important, and this itself is an illusion. The awareness of the ego is the beginning of freedom from it. Silent meditation releases us from the ego-clutch, from its possessiveness, fantasy and illusion. If we make the effort in a positive and constructive way and at the same time learn the uses of silence, we shall fulfil the purpose of the sixth stage of the path. This purpose is fourfold: to remove all evil that is present in the mind; to prevent new evil entering the mind; to develop consistently such good as is already there; and to acquire more good unceasingly. If this fourfold purpose is fulfilled, it will result not only in a deeper wisdom but also in stability and serenity of mind.

This correct effort will not only teach us to appreciate the vows of Gautama, it will help us to become part of their fulfilment. "However innumerable sentient beings may be, I vow to save them; however inexhaustible the defilements of the world may be, I vow to extinguish them; however immeasurable the dharmas are, I vow to master them; and however remote and difficult the goal of enlightenment may be, I vow to attain it".

In the seventh stage we have to discover the foundations of mindfulness. We have to consider the acts and results of meditation. Meditation makes demands upon the meditator. Once the habit is formed, it will be hard to imagine life without it. But the forming of the habit is the real problem. It will be worthwhile spending a fortnight at a school of meditation in order to learn the basic lessons. Everything that is of real value requires time and attention. Even writing and reading should be set aside for the time being. Sometimes the director of meditation will say: "You are the word, you are the book", by which he means that promptings must come from within. These promptings must be tested in solitude and silence. Fasting may be helpful because it reveals discipline and correct priorities. It also gives an opportunity to intensify personal awareness, to consider what it means to keep a meditation vow, and to subdue rival desires.

The meditator should know what he is seeking. He is seeking space within, room to be. This may require giving up a whole day for a period of intensive practice. At first he may pause and relax frequently but later the pauses will be less frequent. Mindfulness means maintaining a conscious awareness of all activities and perceptions. The meditator starts with the awareness of the four postures: sitting, standing, lying down, and going. This means that he has to be aware of the posture presently assumed. The mind gradually becomes calmer and the observation keener. There will be an increasing awareness of all occurrences bodily and mentally as they present themselves. We have just referred to four of the usual activities of man — sitting, standing, lying down, going. Whilst we are aware of what we are doing, we must also be aware of what our action means. Sitting is the posture of enlightenment; standing is the posture of acceptance; lying down is the posture of dying, and going is the posture of becoming. There is no need to spell out the importance of this symbolism for the disclosure will be made to the meditator himself.

If he should know what he is seeking, he should also consciously discern what he is seeing. He will learn to see things as they are and to see them for himself. He will really see them, not seeing merely a facade or what he wants to see. Moreover, he will not be influenced by others' suggestions about what he may see or is expected to see. Discernment, which is a corollary of mindfulness, means to see without being distracted by fantasy, to see something more than an external object, to see why and not just what, and to see the essence rather than the shape or framework. In time the meditator's own experience will become his teacher. Self-reliance, honesty, and a watchful attitude are characteristics of this practice. An illustration may be helpful here. Let us suppose that the object of our meditation is a symbol like a yellow square or a white circle, or a picture or a tree, or perhaps the picture of a boat sailing on a stormy sea. For a few minutes we fix our gaze on it. Then closing our eyes we allow our consciousness to rest on the picture. If the picture fades, we repeat the procedure. The main thing is to note carefully what we see, how long the picture is seen, and what we feel. It may be that the colour of the sea may change, or the boat will appear to move, or the whole picture may cease to be a separate object and become merged into its background. Supposing the picture begins to fade or to float upwards out of sight, what is to be done? Our natural tendency will be to chase after it or become frustrated because it is disappearing. But this would be a mistake. It is better to remain calm and quiet, and perhaps like Abou Ben Adam's angel, it will return. If not, the experience will communicate its own disclosure. It is natural though not always necessary to ask, what is the point of the experience? There may be no obvious meaning. Again it is impossible to quantify the value of the experience. On the other hand, there may be a keener self-understanding, a deep peace, the stormy waves may have turned into a green, waveless sea. Still, there are practical benefits too. The calm of the meditation session will carry over into the rest of the day. Problems may not be removed but will be seen in a different light. It may be that problems not previously seen will appear, but will be seen in proportion. The impact of shocks and irritations will be cushioned by an inner calm and the meditator will be less likely to be goaded into retaliation and self-assertiveness. His thought processes will more easily revolve around a single theme. There may be many other rewards also but at this stage experience will be more important than verbalization.

The principal reward at this stage is the confidence that the pilgrim is on the way to liberation. Of course only Nirvana will bring absolute liberation but it is a great gain to realise that the bonds of self-centredness and ignorance are losing their power. There will follow a sense of total appreciation, a feeling that everything is distinctly good, "everything we look upon is blest". Inner light illumines everything. There will also be an experience of total detachment which produces an objective outlook towards others which enriches all relationships. Total agreeableness follows. For men should avoid being strident and aggressive not only towards each other but towards nature and towards themselves. Whereas in the west a man may refer to the conquest of Everest, in the east he will say, "Everest is my friend and I will make an offering on Mount Kailas".

Mindfulness leads to self-discovery. The mind turns homeward and establishes contact with its creative centre.

To an open house at even home shall men come.

As the weary traveller nears home he thinks not of the many trials that have beset him on his journey but of the peace and bliss that await him. He may somehow feel that all things, even adversities, have conspired to aid him on his journey, for as King Asoka said, "All things that have been rightly said by all the teachers are ours". All things lead to liberation. In the words of the Upanishads: "As the birds fly in the air, as the fish swim in the sea, leaving no traces behind, even so is the pathway to God traversed by the seekers of the spirit".

The Buddha abstained from giving clear-cut answers to metaphysical riddles. He insisted that each one must learn the deepest lessons for himself. The mission of the teacher is to inspire the quest, it is for the pupil to discover the treasure. Each of us has the right and duty of exploring the universe for himself but it does involve finding "that hidden path". Only one stage is left and as with Dante, the hour strikes when Virgil must cease to guide:

> *What reason here discovers, I have power*
> *To show thee; that which lies beyond, expect*
> *From Beatrice, faith not reason's task.*[29]

Before we move on to the last stage of our imaginary journey we must consider the results of mindfulness. The first of these is acceptance. But this quality is positive and not passive. It is really the art of taking the sting out of aggressive force. Things are allowed to take their course without fretting or regret. The results of mindfulness seem almost inevitable. We missed them before but ought to have noticed them. The river flows into the sea. The opening blossom celebrates the sun.

> *A slender branch is covered with snow,*
> *It bends and the snow falls off.*

All this indicates an attitude to life. We should not always resist intellectual difficulties but sometimes allow them to destroy themselves by their own weight. This principle is applied in the eastern art of ju-jitsu; a man allows his opponent to overthrow himself by his own force or weight. The skills of evasion and balance are the mind's response to physical power. The opposing force ministers to its own defeat. The secret is to be utterly involved in life but skilfully to avoid its attacks.

Acceptance brings equanimity. The ability to adapt ourselves to all levels of problems results in equanimity. Lao Tzu illustrates this:

> *Man at his best is like water,*
> *He serves as he goes along;*
> *Like water he seeks his own level,*
> *The common level of life.*[30]

This implies pure effectiveness in which no notion is wasted on outward show. Buddhists quote the following lines as frequently as Taoists partly because they imply the spontaneity and idealism which are implicit in both.

> One may move so well that a footprint never shows,
> Speak so well that the tongue never slips,
> Reckon so well that no counter is needed.[31]

Equanimity allows new insights to appear without protest. The phases and moods of the mind may change but they will not cause disturbance; it is all a matter of patiently watching and waiting. The pool assumes its stillness after the ripples have gone. Meditation is about new insights, fresh visions, and flashes of inspiration. They are "like some bright dream that comes unsought" and they come from the centre of our being. These insights are not dependent on logic or rationalism. As usual it takes a great poet to express what happens when a new insight emerges:

> Light breaks on secret lots,
> On tips of thought where thoughts smell in the rain,
> When logics die,
> The secret of the soil grows through the eye,
> And blood jumps in the sun;
> Above the waste allotment the dawn halts.[32]

Above all there now comes a sense of the order and unity of all things. We are on the path trodden by the Buddhas and the great holy disciples. It brings firmness to our steps if we make the solemn vow made by the one who first trod the path:

> For mind's mastery and growth,
> Effort must be made;
> If once you see the need,
> Why not make it now?
> The road is clearly marked;
> May what I win bring light to me and to all beings.

The eighth stage is the goal of the journey and is best described as the wisdom which brings bliss. Bliss is attained through maturity, suchness and pure consciousness. The wisdom that is attained is the ability to distinguish between suffering and happiness. The Buddha said, "I teach but two things: suffering and release from suffering". For a small child, to be hungry is to suffer, and to be fed is to find release. For the pilgrim on the path, all complicated things are suffering, and the uncomplicated alone is free from suffering. To know the difference between suffering and happiness is liberation, for life consists in the maturing and refining of experience. The path to maturity is a gradual process. The path takes us from infantile dependence, through trial and error, success and failure, to liberated bliss. It must be remembered that each stage of the way must be passed through and no part of it may be by-passed. Great care must be taken not to imagine that we are further ahead than we really are. No one can pass rapidly from the elemental stages to the higher virtues of non-attachment. We reach a stage where everlasting love replaces hatred, acceptance replaces indifference, and faith replaces fear. It is then that the world is no longer seen as over against us, for we ourselves have become part of the unity of all life. Life is like learning a part in a play: we may know our part very well, but we do not understand its significance until we see it in relation to the whole play. Then things hold together and everything begins to make sense. Things previously unknown and unnoticed become significant and things that seem important now appear to be only peripheral to the central meaning.

This central meaning may be described as suchness. Suchness is the essence of everything we see. Everything has an essence, something that makes it what it is in itself, unique and non-transferable. The essence is complete in itself and unchangeable. Even the mind has its essence, a faculty by which everything is assessed. The essence of a chair is a seed, for there could be no chair unless a seed had been planted in the ground. The essence of an oak is an acorn. The essence of a book is an idea and the essence of an action is a motive. An object, therefore, is not to be judged by its shape or function or texture but by its essence. Certain things are essentially right in themselves whatever our opinion may be. Truth, goodness and beauty are self-evident and possess permanent values. We do not add to them by our description, or diminish them by our disregard. Nor do we embellish them by our praise.

Awareness of the essence of an object is an enlightenment.

The way to attain this is by an understanding of the five skandhas. These are qualities which characterise human existence. In *seeing* any object we first notice its external form. The shape conveys a message to our minds and may in turn produce a mental image. Our *feelings* are then brought into play. We may be asked, "What do you feel about it?" rather than, "What do you think about it?" It is natural that there should be an emotional reaction and an artistic appreciation. The third skandha is perception. Further questions arise: Has this shape a meaning and if so, what is its meaning? Is the meaning obvious or obscure? The fourth skandha is connecting, for we must have the ability to relate the object to ourselves. How is it related to us and how is it related to the objects that we see? All these are important, yet we have the ability to see, feel, perceive, and connect only because we have the ability to reflect. Reflection, the fifth skandha, is in its advanced form, meditation. However, the skandhas flatter to deceive. Whilst they are necessary qualities, they are no more than aids to liberation. Just because we see the skandhas coming together and operating in one life, we imagine that we see a separate self. That is our illusion. The skandhas exist to help us see through the illusion, and when that happens, suchness is the result.

Is it possible to describe the experience of suchness? In one sense, it is indescribable. Only guesses are possible. If we meet a person who sees everything as distinctly good, who can look objectively upon his own relationship to others, who can sit quietly by himself, and who has attained an attitude of total agreeableness, such a person has transcended the dividing-line between the finite and the infinite, between life and death, and this is suchness.

It is sometimes said that whatever a man meditates upon, that he obtains. Certainly mysterious powers are often the result of meditation, but the meditator's goal does not concern short-term benefits. He does not expect the satisfaction of a progress chart or the possession of special powers. His goal is always and only final liberation. For this he will freely give up all the rest. This liberation is accompanied by four raptures. The first rapture is the state of joy and peace born of detachment and solitude, even though reason and investigation continue. This is the reward of discipline. The second rapture is a state of joy and peace born of the serenity of concentration, when no reasoning or investigation goes on, and the mind is in a state of elevation and the heart tranquil. This is the reward of patience. The third rapture is the experience in which joy and peace cease to matter, and there arises a subtle but fitful consciousness of the bliss of equanimity. This is the joy of detachment. The fourth rapture is a state of pure consciousness, an experience without pain and without ease. This ultimate bliss is a permanent experience. This is the joy of oneness.

In describing all this we must remember that certain stages of experiences are being passed through simultaneously. The mind is no longer influenced by external agents so that the force of temptation is minimised. The dialectical functions of the mind are suppressed, and concentration follows. The result is a perfect mastery of rarefied consciousness. Now there follows a suspension of relations with the sensible world and with memory. This produces a placid lucidity without any other content than a consciousness of being. Only one further experience now remains; the re-integration of opposites and the bliss of pure consciousness.

References

1. John Masefield, from the poem 'No Highway'.
2. Søren Kierkegaard, *Edifying Discourses*, Fontana, p. 211
3. E. Conze (Ed.), *Buddhist Scriptures*, Penguin, p. 153
4. H. D. Lewis & R. L. Slater, *World Religions*, Watts, p. 70
5. H. C. Warren, *Buddhism in Translation*, p. 146
6. A. J. Saunders, *The Development of Religious Thought in India*, Christian Literature Society, pp. 162-3
7. G. A. Studdert Kennedy, *The Unutterable Beauty*, Hodder
8. H. C. Warren, *Buddhism in Translation*, pp. 76-83
9. W. Macquity, *Buddhism*, p. 40
10. J. Hayward, (Ed.), *The Faber Book of English Verse*, from the poem 'I am' by John Clare, Faber, p. 305
11. J. W. Von Goethe, (Trans: B. Taylor), *Faust*, Houghton Mifflin, pp. 14, 28
12. Lin Yutang, (Ed.), *The Wisdom of China*, Random House, New York, p. 479
13 Matthew Arnold, *Matthew Arnold's Poetical Works*, Macmillan, p. 306
14a H. V. Guenther, *Buddhist Philosophy in Theory and*
& 14b *Practice*, Viking Penguin Inc., New York, pp. 43, 45
15. Martin Buber, *The Knowledge of Man*, Routledge & Kegan Paul. See also *Between Man and Man*, p. 20, Fontana.
16. C. Humphreys, *The Search Within*, Sheldon, p. 32
17. T. S. Eliot, *Four Quartets*, Faber and Faber, p. 58
18. Bhikkhu Silicara, *The Noble Eightfold Path*, p. 25
19. Martin Buber, *Response*, p. 308
20. H. Saddhatissa, *The Buddha's Way*, Unwin, p. 50
21. A. C. Bouquet, *Sacred Books of the World*, from the Katha Upanishad, Pelican, p. 127
22. S. Cave, cited in *Hinduism or Christianity*, Hodder, p. 71
23. Buddhist Society Publication, *What is Buddhism?* p. 111
24. H. Saddhatissa, *The Buddha's Way*, ('samma ajiva' means 'a correct means of livelihood'), Unwin, p. 53
25. W. Johnston, *Silent Music*, Collins, p. 56

26. Rabindranath Tagore, *Gitanjali* LX, Macmillan
27. Rabindranath Tagore, *Gitanjali* XLIV, Macmillan
28. Monica Furlong, *Contemplating Now*, Hodder, p. 59
29. Dante (Trans: M. B. Anderson), *Divine Comedy* Vol II, Oxford, pp. 18, 47-48
30. Lao Tsu (Trans: R. B. Blakney), *The Way of Life*, Mentor, p. 8
31. *Ibid*, p. 21
32. Dylan Thomas, *Collected Poems*, David Higham Associates Ltd

The Christian Way

The Christian Way

Is there a Way?

The Way from the Father

The Way to the Father

The Way of Compassion

The Way of Salvation

Followers of the Way

Is there a Way?

The first thing to do is to set this question in its philosophical context. Some will want to question whether there is a Way at all. So we must ask how this sceptical attitude has arisen. The question 'Is there a Way' is more likely to arise in the western world than in the Orient. Critical questions will arise in the Orient but this will usually happen within the ambit of religious belief. This is because all philosophy in the eastern world is the philosophy of religion. In the west there is a very articulate school of secular philosophy and this may have some advantages because religious ideas will be subjected to the sharp edge and discipline of philosophical enquiry. But sometimes in their eagerness to attack religious ideas some philosophers have tried to prove too much and their doctrines have boomeranged on them.

Linguistic philosophers have generally adopted a condescending attitude to religion and their arrogance has prevented them from realising that their doctrine was, as Ernest Gellner called it, 'an implausible Bluebird'.[1] This means that it was an over-simplistic generalisation and hardly more than a repetition of the problem put forward by Logical Positivism. This maintained that philosophy was no longer about theories of the world or moral values but about meaning and language and the recording of facts. So those truths which help many people to make sense of their lives — moral and political principles, ethical concepts, religious beliefs and evaluations of all kinds, were swept aside at a stroke. Although the influence of linguistic philosophy has faded considerably during the last two decades, it has left the impression that what religion offers is bogus knowledge. The case against religious statements is that they are not verifiable by sensory perception and, therefore, are classed as nonsense or as mere emotive utterances which can neither be confirmed nor refuted. Actually the claim that the meaning of a proposition depends upon the method of its verification is itself an assumption. So according to linguistic philosophy's own principles, it is nonsense. It follows that all the armoury brought against religious ideas must also be directed against the verification principle which is itself a metaphysical concept. It does not record facts or calculations, and since it states a principle similar to moral and religious principles, by the same token it is meaningless.

In any case philosophy does not concern language alone. Words are important but to confine the problem to words alone is to reduce philosophy to grammar. Philosophy deals with concepts, evaluations, problems of intention, purpose and command, it is not just about facts and figures. It is too simplistic a generalisation to say that all knowledge comes through the sensations, and it is high time the ghost was laid. We have to include *a priori* knowledge, intuition, memory, allegory, extra-sensory perception and revelation. To overlook these is to neglect a large slice of human experience.

In addition to the philosophical assault on religion we must now turn to the historical question. Does it matter whether Jesus really lived? Can we believe in his teaching without believing in him as a person? Is the Sermon on the Mount sufficient for our salvation? To some minds the tie-up with historical facts seems either unnecessary or foolish. Mahatma Gandhi, for instance, wrote as follows: 'I may say I have never been interested in a historical Jesus. I should not care if it was proved by someone that the man called Jesus never lived, and that what was narrated in the Gospels was a figment of the writer's imagination'.[2] It is not only in the East that this problem has arisen. Lowes Dickinson, the classical scholar, has said: 'My difficulty about Christianity is, and always has been, that Christians make the essence of their faith the historical existence of a man at a certain age. I dare say he did exist, though that has been doubted. But if he did, what was he really like? I cannot think that religion can depend upon such un-certainties'.[3]

However, the Gospel records — text, authenticity and

historicity, have been subjected to a strict examination which is not normally applied to other literary works. One of the foremost among Form Critics, Dr. Vincent Taylor, declared many times that the Christian religion was rooted in the black soil of history. The statement is profoundly important, a man who never really lives never really dies. While the Sermon on the Mount is an impressive ethical guide, it does not contain either the means or the offer of salvation. It represents one aspect of the Christian Faith, not the whole of it.

Another challenge is made by the humanist who appears to want Christian ethics without Christ. Further he dislikes the link between Christianity and the God of the Old Testament and demurs at the idea of unqualified submission and obedience. 'The Christian must remain concentrated upon and bound by the example of Christ as the supreme example for human living. Now Christ as a human personality is an enigma, but as a standard and pattern there is no doubt or obscurity about him: he is the archetype of unqualified submission and obedience to the will of God, the God of Abraham and of Isaac and of Jacob. It is impossible to follow Christ on any other terms and the humanist finds acceptance of these terms a violation of himself and his whole experience. His rejection of Christ is therefore categorical: he can do no other. There is no separation of Christian ethics from the particular faith of which Christ is the supreme exemplar'.[4] It is hard to see why 'unqualified submission' is an obstacle when the quotation is taken from one who is totally committed to Humanism. Christianity offers man hope and liberation which is also what the humanist seeks to do. The difference lies in the way in which this liberation is achieved. The dimension of Humanism is included in the Christian position. On the whole, Christianity fully approves of the virtues implicit in Humanism but claims to add something more. It maintains that holiness is man's ultimate aim and this is possible only with divine help.

Many people extend a sentimental approval to the Christian religion but even this is not enough. 'Will great originality be born again, or will the world content itself henceforth by the bold creators of the ancient ages? We know not. But whatever may be the unexpected phenomena of the future, Jesus will not be surpassed. His worship will constantly renew its youth, the tale of his life will cause ceaseless tears, his suffering will soften the best hearts; all the ages will proclaim that among the sons of men there is none born who is greater than Jesus'.[5] This is a noble tribute but it lacks one important element: allegiance to the one whose virtues it extols. Renan thought that the teaching of Jesus was original and that his character was unsurpassable but he still withheld that belief which would have given the deepest significance to his words. It is one thing to say that Jesus will 'soften the best hearts' but it is quite another to say that he demands personal faith and lifelong obedience.

There is little doubt that there is something in the compassionate character of Jesus which makes a strong appeal to Hindus but they wish to go back to the simplicity of Christian beginnings. They believe that the superstructure of ecclesiastical organisation has become so top heavy that the true function of Christianity has become obscured. Gandhi's question haunts us all: 'Where is the Carpenter in this massive demonstration of power?' Tagore's advice should be heeded if only because it was exemplified in his own life: 'Do not be always trying to preach your doctrine but give yourself in love'. Jesus appeals to Hindus as the Nazarene Sannyasi. Born in a stable where the beasts are his companions and the simple shepherds his devotees, Jesus begins his life as one who had no certain dwelling-place. Nature was his temple and the stars his canopy. One short narrative breaks the silence of many preparatory years and this presents the picture of one whose mind is already set on the things of God: 'Know ye not that I must be about my Father's business?' Some eighteen years later when he is introduced to us again, he is attached to a wandering prophet, a true ascetic who is dressed in skins and lives on fruit and wild honey, and who spends his days and nights in the Jordan valley. How closely is the world of nature associated with those early scenes! A voice comes out of the cloud, a dove descends upon him, and the river is the scene of his baptism. Then, as is the case with the true Sannyasi, 'the Spirit driveth him into the wilderness' where he wrestles with the Tempter. And do not their own Sadhus spend many days and nights in the wilderness deep in meditation, and are they not seeking victory over material things and the peace that is not of this world? Even so Hindus seem contented with Jesus the Sannyasi. He is the wisest, bravest, holiest of mankind, but still 'of mankind'. They have succeeded in humanising the Jesus they are able to understand but the Lord and Saviour of the world eludes them. Tender and loving as Jesus is, he does not merely offer words of comfort. To meet him is to be aware of a crisis in which important decisions must be made. The first disciples realised that the most vital issue of their lives was to take up a specific attitude to the Master and that this involved a life-long commitment.

We have noticed how the agnostic approach to Christian ideas was prompted by linguistic philosophers and we have considered the words of a renowned Hindu idealist, a western classical scholar, a modern humanist, and a French philosopher and historian. All of them express doubts about the historical reliability of Christianity and all of them appear to concentrate their attention on the founder of the faith. The question at issue seems to be: Is there a true and living way and is this way clearly expressed in the life, teaching and triumph of Jesus himself? In endeavouring to answer this question we shall consider the evidence of the New Testament and enquire whether the one who emerges from its pages qualifies to be Saviour and Lord and therefore the pioneer of a new and living way. And to this consideration we must now turn. Maybe the exposition which follows will do something to explain or answer the doubts, criticisms and questions which have been mentioned here.

The Christian Way

When the late Archbishop William Temple visited Wesley College, Headingley, in 1938 to address the students he chose as his subject, 'The need for a Christocentric metaphysic'. It can be stated with some assurance that not all the students understood the title, still less the address. They need not have been too anxious because it was clear from the address that the subject was still in the process of formation in the speaker's mind. Still, the idea was on the drawing board and perhaps Dr Temple did more than most to give a philosophical interpretation to traditional Christology. Strangely enough it is frequently the philospher who emphasises the divine side of reality while the theologian is preoccupied in explaining the human side. However, the pendulum swings from one side to the other at least twice in a century.

It is hardly possible to discuss the concept of the Way in the Christian religion without the prior realisation that the founder of Christianity is himself the Way. He is the Way from the Father, the Way to the Father, the Way of Compassion, the Way of Salvation, and those who believe in him are known as 'Followers of the Way'. Each of these phrases must now be carefully examined.

The Way from the Father

The oft-repeated statement that 'Jesus is just like us' immediately prompts the question, 'Like which of us?' It is not merely that in many respects he is different from us but that his relationship with the religion he founded is unique. There is no Christianity without Christ. It is sometimes argued that if a religion contains sublime truths, it scarcely matters whether the original teacher ever lived. The theory is interesting but unacceptable. The teacher embodies the teaching and the teaching explains the teacher. Whatever is proclaimed in the gospel is directly or indirectly about Christ. If we define the gospel as the love of God in action, we are also describing the role of Christ. So teacher and teaching are inseparable. Christ does not only point the way, he is the Way. He does not merely receive a revelation, he is the revelation.

There is considerable interest in these days in 'pilgrim theology'. It refers to theology which is always open to new understandings of divine revelation. A living theology must be a pilgrim theology, an activity of those who are on the way in both life and thought. It indicates an open stance, an approximation to truth rather than its final expression. Generally speaking, pilgrims are on the way to the goal but have not yet arrived. They are travelling from the earthly city to the heavenly. But sometimes the usual rules do not apply and a pilgrim comes from the other direction. It is not simply that one pilgrim, taking his courage in both hands, moves ahead of all the others, but rather that he approaches them from a different direction. He is first and foremost the Way from the Father. It is important to emphasise this difference of direction. The saints and sages, the priests and prophets, and all the great religious of the past, have moved in the same direction. Christ reverses the process.

This implies that he brings truths which belong to another dimension. They have a divine source rather than a human one. We have the task of explaining him even though his character is enigmatic and mysterious. The Jews are by no means the only ones who have found it difficult to assess his importance. Some modern Jews believe that messiahship is a concept which takes aeons to achieve. But Jesus was impatient and refused to wait. Out of a long line of self-appointed messiahs he appeared to be the only one who stepped out of line, arrogating messiahship to himself. Because he spoke out of turn, the Jews could not recognise him. In any case the world is still unredeemed, so how can it be claimed that the redeemer has come?

Of course it has to be remembered that the pronouncements of some of his early followers, themselves Jews, pointed in the direction of messiahship. At least they recognised that Jesus had a special relationship with, and a special mission from, the Father. He came from the Father and was unable to do anything without the Father's approval. He was the servant of the

Father's will and spoke only the words that his Father had commanded. Yet this affinity did not lead him to claim equality but to renounce it. The case was made for him by the pronouncements of his followers. Yet even the disciples could not grasp everything, for human comprehension has its limits.

Christ stood before them inherently divine and the reality of his divinity disclosed itself in human form. Yet even when they had exhausted every possible way of describing him, their words fell short of the reality. They might have said as Augustine said much later, 'Can any man say everything when he speaks of you?'[6] The limitation was in their comprehension rather than in their master's revelation. At regular intervals some aspect or other of Christology is re-emphasized and this in itself is a tribute to the many-sided character whom scholars try to describe and explain. To categorise such a person is impossible and perhaps unnecessary. When all attempts at explanation have been made, there is still a certain differentia that is left unexplained. So the age-old question confronts us again: in what sense is Jesus different?

He is different in what he says. It is significant that religions are often represented by rituals, regulations and pilgrimages. When requiring advice or guidance or inspiration, people are instructed to do this, read that or go there. Sometimes they are asked to visit a sacred shrine or make a pilgrimage to a sacred city. They may be instructed to visit a temple or bathe in a sacred river. However, the statement of Jesus to his followers is astonishing in its simplicity. It is possible to miss its authority because of its simplicity. He said, 'Come unto me'. The world had waited a long time for someone who had the right as well as the courage to utter these words. For here we have invitation and command, promise and direction all in one. Jesus does not refer his followers to other people or places or events. He knew no more sacred duty than pointing men to himself. Yet if the invitation were all-inclusive, so was the result of a ready response, 'I will give you rest'. All mankind yearns to hear the calm assurance of these words. Does the offer of this rest refer to the end of the pilgrimage? It means rather a reassessment of its meaning, a continuation of the search at a deeper level.

Rest is the inward peace consequent upon forgiveness. It imparts a strange freedom and joy for which every believer yearns. Free from the nagging anxiety about his own salvation, he is now at liberty to serve others, to pray for them and inspire them on their pilgrimage.

If Jesus is different in what he says, he is also different in what he does. Most great leaders seek power but there is a difference between the kind of power they seek and the use they make of it. Usually people seek power in order to rule or to achieve their purpose or to control others or perhaps to wield great influence. Power is often regarded as the answer to most questions, social or political. It is customary, for instance, to speak of military, political or industrial power. Jesus, however, was not interested in the kind of power that is associated with great armies or with the attainment of wealth or influence. He was concerned with a different kind of power. He believed in the power of example, of moral influence, of those mysterious energies whose source is the Spirit. One of the early tests which came to him was concerned with the nature of the power he was to wield. He was asked to believe that one spectacular miracle might impress men providing the timing was right. If he made a show of temporal power, perhaps he could end oppression at once. It was not wrong to end oppression but it was wrong to do so by becoming a slave to those forces which caused oppression in the first place. The Pharaohs and the Caesars had shown pomp and power and opportunism in abundance. Was Jesus to use their methods as well as their temporal power? He knew that he must not coerce men by a show of omnipotence. That would have been to use the method of the tyrant throughout the ages. As far as Jesus was concerned the right moment for such a method was never. He knew that men must be won and not coerced by over-whelming power. Not only did Jesus emphasise a different kind of power but he made it clear that it should be used for a different purpose. He possessed that spiritual power which is the servant of love. Moreover, he always used his power to produce hope. His promise to his disciples, 'I will see you again and your hearts shall rejoice',[7] was evidence both of the power he exercised and of the hope the disciples needed. In this connection his two statements before Pilate are of paramount significance: 'I have power to lay down my life and to take it up again'.[8] Nor did he hesitate to say to Pilate, the representative of imperial power: 'You have no power unless it were given you from above'.[9] Christians have not been slow to grasp the importance of these statements. After all, what man has the power to loosen the chains of death? And what man, having risen, raises everyone with him?

Jesus is different in what he gives. His gifts are distinctive. He offers his teaching, his life, his spirit, forgiveness and eternal life. Can he complete the work God has given him to do? The answer to this question is crucial for the future of the Christian religion. Everything seemed to depend upon his relationship with his disciples. Let us notice the threefold legacy mentioned in John 20. 'Receive ye the Holy Spirit'; 'Peace be unto you'; 'As the Father has sent me, so send I you'. Three basic essentials of Christianity are included here. Only by receiving his spirit could they become vehicles of his power. Only by receiving his peace could they offer this incomparable blessing to the world. Only by receiving his commission had they the right and authority to communicate his message to others. We must not overlook the importance of these statements for the power which he possessed and the works which he wrought. He has no abiding place, no possessions, no house nor home, yet he holds in trust the one power which can transform the world. So he offers the one gift which all men need, the spirit of Christ.

If Jesus is different in what he gives, it is because he is different in what he is. It is true that his name divides history and that he has given his name to our era. If he divides history horizontally, he introduces a new vertical dimension as well. He brings a new quality of life which can only be regarded as divine. Truly he comes from a different direction but that is not all: entering the world, wherever he goes he pioneers a new way. He traversed a way which had been previously unknown. He received and accepted and achieved all that the Father had planned for him. He acknowledged his dependence on the Father. He was always obedient to the Father's commands and was vividly aware of his universal mission to the world.

Such a person has to be reckoned with. It is scarcely possible to avoid this responsibility. Consider the following statements, one from the New Testament, and the other from modern times: Simeon waited in the temple to welcome a mother and child, and looking on the child's face said, 'Now let thy servant depart in peace, for mine eyes have seen thy salvation'.[10] It was enough, for in that child he had seen both the promise and guarantee of salvation. The second incident took place in India. Narayan Tilak casually picked up a Bible which had been left on a berth in a railway carriage. He read some words from the gospels and later remarked, 'I could not tear myself away from those burning words of compassion and love'. Similar experiences have been recorded in all the intervening centuries.

In his earthly days no one doubted that Jesus was a real person. They might question how he was unique but not that he was unique. No one doubted that he possessed a certain power over evil; they might question the use he made of it but not his inherent power. No one doubted that astonishing effects resulted from his words and deeds. His presence was enough to change situations. There were great expectations whenever he appeared, for he seemed to possess inexhaustible powers. No one doubted that if there was such a thing as immortality, it must be connected with him. Words fell from his lips which stunned his hearers, words like 'I am the resurrection',[11] but his deeds confirmed the reality of his words. Death may still remain a mystery but the anxiety has been reduced because the sting of fear has been removed. Christ pioneers a way which passes through death to resurrection life.

The reduction of this anxiety is considerable. What Christ has done he has done once and for all. It cannot be undone and need never be repeated. Whatever happens in the future will complement what he said but it will not change it. All sorts and conditions of men in every place and in any age may reflect that they are the recipients of the benefits and blessings that Christ has won. No one is left out. Everyone is entitled to rely on the merits of our Redeemer. The effects of his life, death and victory will not be erased from human history. Even if all our descriptions fall short, their very failure is a tribute to him whose glory cannot be fully expressed.

The Way to the Father

Jesus came from the Father and therefore is qualified to lead mankind to the Father.[12] He had to know the way before he could show the way.[13] The first thing Jesus had to do was to tackle the question of fear. To portray God as judge is to paint only half the picture. Many Christian thinkers of the past have had a desperate struggle to disabuse their minds of a deep-seated belief in God as judge. God is judge but also something more: 'a righteous God and a saviour'.[14] God is powerful but for what purpose does he use his power? There may be historical and psychological reasons why the human race has harboured the most fearsome ideas of God but ought these ideas to be perpetually proclaimed? Zeus, Yahweh, Brahma and Allah have been depicted as hostile, selfish, vindictive and remote. Clearly such ideas must be corrected, for if they remain, man's struggle is without hope. He will always be defeated in the contest with gods who seem hostile and vengeful. The struggle will be uneven and the contest too heavily weighted against man.

It is at this point that Jesus works something of a revolution. He gives to mankind a joyous idea of God. The question is: is God approachable, gracious and compassionate? The answer of Jesus is an unequivocal 'yes'. He uses the Aramaic word 'Abba' to illustrate his intimate relationship with the Father. Far from being sentimental, this idea enabled people to turn towards God in hope rather than in despair. The use of the word 'Abba' breaks the barriers of distance, hostility, fear and taboo. The change which this brought in man's approach to God was so dramatic as to be almost indescribable. Rarely has a single word effected so deep a change in human attitudes. So wherein does its significance lie? For one thing, prior to the New Testament there is no instance of this word being used in prayer to God. The word implies an intimacy with God which presumably would have been inconceivable outside Christian circles. It signifies not so much a recognition of authority as a loving personal relationship. Moreover, Christians took over the word and used it to show their own close relationship with God as his children. They dared to use it as they found themselves accepted and adopted into the family of God.[15]

Some of the teaching of Jesus was no doubt based on rabbinic stories. Some parables, for instance, have parallels in the stories of the rabbis, but the originality of this joyous idea of God is beyond question. The consequence is that people may now approach God with confidence, hope and joy. Coming from the Father, he reveals the character of the Father. Not only is Jesus the way to the Father but he pioneers the way for everyone else. The idea is not only unique, it is the first step in man's salvation, for a gracious Father will take action on behalf of those who turn to him.

Jesus stands facing God with a high responsibility for all those who stand behind him. Their confidence is strengthened because they know whence he has come and trust him to lead them along the way he knows. There is no point in claiming that there is nothing enigmatic about the life and work of Jesus. Sometimes he creates a stir only to play it down. He causes people to shout hallelujah and then raises a doubt. He asks a question and then refuses to answer it. He seems to agree about his divine status and then dies on the cross. His followers had to work it out for themselves. If they were puzzled about where to place Jesus in the scheme of things, so are we. What sort of person was he? A saintly man? a fervent nationalist? a wandering prophet? a great teacher in the rabbinic tradition? a martyr or the Son of God in human form? In answer to these questions we can at least make some important affirmations. Even if we cannot describe him in detail, we can assess the impression that he made upon his followers. He was a Jewish carpenter living in Galilee.[16] He was not a scholar in the professional sense, nor a rabbi, nor a member of the upper class, but a man who worked for a living with his hands and supported the family. He came across to his companions as a man of human feelings whose emotions were sometimes difficult to control. He was uncompromising in putting into practice the things he believed in. His followers were not slow to confess the faith he taught. They believed in him, said so and were willing to pay the price of their convictions.

The writer to the Hebrews tells us that 'He was made like unto his brethren'.[17] This means that his was a really human life. Many gods and goddesses have appeared from time to time but of which of them can it be said, 'the child grew'? He was born a child and learned by the experiences he passed through. He grew to be the man he was by obedience, discipline and responsibility. The New Testament shows that he was subject to those human limitations without which he could not be truly man. Sometimes he was tired, surprised, and sorrowful. He confessed that there were some things that he did not know.[18] Requiring information he asked many questions. Nor was he immune from temptation.[19] He was particularly adept at helping people to respond.[20] He repeatedly appealed to their own insight.[21] His answers were often in the form of questions.[22] He had a warm welcome for a ready response.[23] Yet he patiently waited for them to discover new truths for themselves and did not forestall their discoveries. He gave them broad principles and left them to apply them in their own lives.[24] Even his silences were significant. When asked by Caiaphas, 'Are you a king then?' he remained silent. The implication was that they should draw their own conclusions. The cumulative evidence of this is impressive as also are the conclusions reached by those who met him. Their witness is spontaneous and clear: 'Is not this the Christ?'[25] From the one who had to pronounce judgment upon him: 'Behold the man'.[26] And from a Roman guard: 'Beyond all doubt, this was an innocent man'.[27] The general consensus was 'No one could perform these works unless God were with him'.[28]

The sole concern of Jesus was that the follower should be aware of what God was doing. He himself does only what he sees the Father doing.[29] This means that he saw the Father doing something. It is possible to live in the world and not see the Father doing anything. Jesus encouraged people to be aware of God's activity. Yet even when people see these signs

the cry goes up 'intervention, coincidence, the supernatural!'
Contrast this with the attitude of Jesus: he expected God to be
doing something. He saw God's action everywhere. He saw it in
the beauty of the lilies and the cornfield's waving gold. He saw
it in the gentle rain and in the joy of harvest. He saw it in the
faces of children and in all acts of compassion, healing and
understanding. Alas! it is all too easy for people to see without
perceiving what he perceived.

Jesus also wanted his followers to see that what God was
doing was perfect and right. He wanted to know that if only
they could see God's ways, they could not endure any other.
Jesus lived in a world where the Father lived and worked and
in that world he found not only his role but his blessedness.
Jesus made room for God to do his work. He showed us that
God was prepared to lose something of himself in order to
become identified with us. 'There is a tale that a man inspired
by God once went out from the creaturely realms into the vast
waste. There he wandered till he came to the gates of the
mystery. He knocked. From within came the cry: "What do
you want here?" He said, "I have proclaimed your praise in the
ears of mortals, but they were deaf to me. So I came to you
that you yourself may hear me and reply". "Turn back," came
the cry from within. "Here is no ear for you. I have sunk my
hearing in the deafness of mortals".[30] There is just the chance
that in the hurry and bustle of everyday life as people grope
past one another, they may almost accidentally touch the one
who will help them make contact with the eternal partner.
Certainly their Lord is there helping them to be aware of God's
action in their midst and in doing this he found harmony of
work as well as harmony of will. Possibly this was one of the
secrets that he wished to impart.

> Thou didst live to God alone;
> Thou didst never seek thine own:
> Thou thyself didst never please;
> God was all thy happiness.[31]

If the Father's work was perfect and right, then the Son
must do nothing of which the Father would not approve. Here

is another vital lesson to impart to those who seek the way to the Father. The Son's first decision after his baptism was a refusal to do certain things because they were not God's way. He could not turn stones into bread (though this was not a base thing to do) without first asking why God had not done it or made it unnecessary long before. Jesus knew the answer: men must be won, not bought. Nor could he use worldly means to establish heavenly rule. His appeal was different from the usual ones. He appealed to men's own insight and insisted that they should see the truth for themselves. He began with each man where that man was, asking first and last that men should be sincere and open with him and assuring them that if they would look and listen, they would see and understand. In all this he received the Father's approval for 'angels came and ministered unto him'.[32]

If Jesus did what the Father approved, he believed that this would have a good effect, perhaps even a transforming effect, upon the world. He taught that our relations with one another are inextricably involved in our relation with God. We cannot love God unless we love our brother also. We cannot have mercy from God and then refuse it to our brother. We cannot have God's forgiveness and then compel others to buy our forgiveness at a price. If we thus turn our back on our fellows, we turn our back on God. In the one picture given us of the final judgment all judgment turns on one thing — compassion. The damning thing is to be in a world of need and not to recognise it. So it is not too much to claim that the Christian Way as portrayed by Jesus is first and foremost a way of compassion.

The Way of Compassion

One thing had to be made clear from the start, he would have no truck with Satan. History was strewn with instances of good men who had chosen false means to achieve laudable ends. The story of his own race was no exception. In the third temptation which came to him he was invited to do a deal with Satan. Like Faust he was tempted to sell his soul to the devil. He might gain the kingdoms of the world by compromising his position. But what was the point of winning kingdoms if he forfeited human souls? In any case, to worship Satan is to dethrone God. But the aim of Jesus was to enthrone God in the universe and in the hearts of men. Had he failed on this single issue, his whole programme would have been in ruins. It is one thing to proclaim a sublime message but a very different thing to make it work in the circumstances of a rebellious world. It is one thing to say that God is love and another thing to demonstrate it in every gesture and action and sacrifice.

In more senses than one the Incarnation is the turning point, or more accurately the turning-round point. The way from the Father had been travelled, and now stands Jesus facing the Father and committed to the awesome task of bringing all mankind back to the Father. But how? Jesus was responsible for showing that the world was the scene of God's activity. Not that this is the only reason for the existence of the physical universe, but it is one reason and not an unimportant one. The divine plan could not exist in a vacuum. It had to be interpreted and fulfilled in the context of this world. It was not a blue-print for heaven but for earth. Jesus accepted the natural world as God's world and revealed God's meaning in it. For him the whole creation was sacramental. The outward and visible world corresponded with the inward and spiritual one. God's beauty and care and constancy are seen in the natural world as well as in human life.

> *Father, 'tis thine each day to yield*
> *Thy children's wants a fresh supply;*
> *Thou cloth'st the lilies of the field,*
> *And hearest the young ravens cry.*[33]

The New Testament teaches us to go to all lengths to love even our enemies. How could Jesus make good that sort of teaching? He does not merely quote laws or authorities or books, he introduces his own criteria. He simply tells us to look and see how God treats his enemies: 'He makes his sun to shine on the evil and the good'.[34] In this way the sun becomes a lamp of reconciliation. Again, Jesus points us to a sovereign remedy for care. He tells us to look at the birds, the flowers and the soil, and to learn our lessons there. But he did not just see these things, he saw God taking care of them. The whole universe was saying to God's estranged children: 'Be ye reconciled to God'.[35]

However, sometimes the Christian attitude to nature has been too vague. The lessons are there in the Psalms (19 and 47) and in Isaiah 40 but St. Paul, for instance, says little about the ceaseless ministries of nature. 'Does God care for oxen?[36] and implies that the answer is 'no'. St Augustine takes a different point of view: 'Good is the earth with its lofty mountains, its gentle hills, its level plains. Good is the beauteous and fertile land, good the well-built house with its symmetry, its spaciousness and light. Good are the bodies of living things, good is the temperate and wholesome air, good is the pleasant and healthful food, good is health itself free from pain and weariness'.[37] Again in the teaching of St Francis we see a universe that is friendly and co-operative and sacramental. Sometimes this aspect of God's revelation to man has been overlooked. When this happens man is guilty of an inexcusable blind spot. For God has shown us in nature a pattern of order and beauty and care. Jesus was aware of what was going on around him and it was God's activity that was going on. He accepted the conditions of human life and revealed God's meaning there. The way to the Father is along our earthly and human way. Along this road all may find signs of love and compassion:

> *It is a sun-baked road,*
> *And those who tread it find*
> *The footprints of a traveller*
> *With love upon his mind.*

In travelling this earthly road Jesus faced hard tasks and many uncertainties and frustrations. He accepted the disciplines imposed upon him. Born as a child in a family, he carried memories of his childhood into later life. His schooldays were a necessary preparation for later tasks as were his years as a carpenter.

Where Joseph plies his trade,
There Jesus labours too,
The hands that all things made,
An earthly craft pursue.[38]

None of these human experiences was alien to him, and each played an important part in making him what he was. Although there was an ascetical element in the character of Jesus, this never made him cynical about the world. Far from leaving it to its own fate, he accepts it and leads it through darkness and death to a light that does not fade.

Jesus accepted a normal environment, entering into social relationships and seeing in them a divine significance. Yet in many of those human relationships sooner or later he was let down. Religious leaders, his closest disciples, those whom he had healed and befriended, and even members of his own family, failed him. Yet he never repudiated any of these relationships, and although the moral distances between him and others were great, he put himself on and at their side. He prayed for his enemies, not against them. He urged that this should be their attitude as well. All this applies to his followers today. He taught us that God has done many things for us in which we ought to rejoice. He has given us our moral freedom and thereby made it possible for us to be his children, not his machines, puppets or slaves. This has placed upon us the necessity of choice, responsible conduct and the acceptance of consequences.

Consider the following parable. Suppose God through an angel said to us: 'See, here are two worlds; choose which one you will enter. If you enter this one you shall neither be helped nor hurt by anyone's deeds or misdeeds save your own. You shall carry your own burden but no other, your own joy but no other. Nothing that men call "undeserved" shall ever come your way. But if you enter the other one, you come into a family that is in trouble, and your joy must be the family joy. You shall reap in joy and sorrow where others have sown. You are promised no immunity from the consequences of other people's sins, neglects or ignorances, nor they from yours. Only this you may have: that God has chosen to be of this family and he is always to be found there'. If we choose the second, what is the ground of our complaints? For instance, we get more than our share of trouble and less than our share of joy. But all of it is shared with God and with others.

If we accept the conditions mentioned in the parable we begin to see that faith in Christ must include faith in the things he stood for. There seems no other way. In one sense he cannot save us unless he is free to make us like himself. For not even God can give us peace in things that are not true, or happiness in things that are not good. There are commands that are too difficult and there are aspects of our salvation that we do not understand. There are also experiences that seem to hinder rather than help us. The secret is not simply to know Christ's values, ideas and commands, but to get to know him. If we can see everything in the light of what he is, we shall learn to see them as they really are.

Is it all that difficult to appreciate this truth? God has put us in a sacramental world where all things speak of him. Sometimes we do not listen, our receivers have been turned off. Even when we listen, we take no heed. When good opportunities come, we have fallen so far behind in perception and understanding that we have become almost impervious to truth. But God comes to people in different ways, and he has his own ways of letting us know his mind. Most religious experiences constitute a response to the sacramental world. A vision, an inner voice, a perfect flower, a call to obedience, may teach us more about ourselves than we ever knew. But if any one of these experiences shows us a way to the Father, it is all we need to know.

The Way of Salvation

Three stories will help us place this subject in its true context. Each tells us in a different way that something is lost which must be recovered.

Father, mother, and their two sons lived in the most pleasant

surroundings. Their own orchards and fields amply supplied
their material needs. There was an abundance of trees, fruits
and flowers, a wide river and an impressive view of distant hills.
Everything seemed to ensure security and happiness. They
wanted for nothing and their environment might be described
as a sort of paradise. One stark sentence marred the serene
bliss of this idyllic scene. 'Cain attacked his brother Abel and
murdered him'.[39]

'There was a small town with few inhabitants, and a great
king came to attack it; he besieged it and constructed great
siege-works against it. There was in it a poor wise man, and he
alone might have saved the town by his wisdom, but no one
remembered that poor wise man'.[40]

'In the beginning Liberty, Equality and Fraternity went
hand in hand. Then their paths divided. Liberty turned towards
the West, but changed its nature on the way. Equality turned
towards the East; but it also changed during this journey. No
one knows what happened to Fraternity. It seems to have been
lost . . . Now Liberty and Equality would like to rejoin one
another and become what they were in the beginning. But they
cannot do this unless we find Fraternity again'.

There is no need to elaborate on the meaning of these
stories. The tragedy in each carries its own significance. Our
race has somehow managed to lose innocence, wisdom and
fraternity. Is there any place where they can be re-discovered?
It is not difficult to state some of the assets of our age. We
have not lacked imagination, having formed a European
Community so that traditional enemies may seek the paths of
peace. We have not lacked inventiveness, having explored outer
space and even reached the moon. We have not lacked courage,
having conquered Everest, crossed the Atlantic in an air balloon
and explored the teeming life of the oceans. But with all our
successes we still seem woefully deprived. Ideologies become
dividing walls and ideas of liberation end up in labour camps.
Even Olympic ideals serve to accentuate political rivalries. Just
as one part of the world surrenders its imperial aims, another
part eagerly adopts them. Whatever man touches he seems to
corrupt. Race, religion, politics and industry tend to divide or

destroy. We are bedevilled by vandalism, violence and the spirit of revenge. All kinds of remedies have been tried and found wanting. Legislation, financial aid, progressive education, race commissions, social welfare, and lighter sentences, all have been tried but the answer to our problems still eludes us. One thing at least is clear about the twentieth century: we have had the apocalyptic signs without the apocalyptic salvation.

An examination of the symptoms may sometimes help to identify the cause. In troublous times people often look for compensatory factors. When things go against them they must compensate by going against someone else. This turns out to be another way of saying that an individual is entitled to even out life's injustices by means of his own devising. Boredom has become the most common excuse for petty crime. But boredom is not a reason, it is refusal to give a reason. Because this feeling of boredom is not faced rationally, it reaches an explosive point. A lost soccer match triggers an attack on rival fans. Such rebound emotionalism is one of the sad characteristics of our society. In order to give some kind of explanation for these events people look around for a scapegoat. Any scapegoat will do so long as it can be generalised. Now it is the Police or the 'system' or the government or the immigrants or the older generation or the younger or even the Common Market. The accusing finger always points outward to something or someone else.

However, to look for a scapegoat is no more than a form of escapism. An alternative to escapism is belief in nihilism which is sometimes the logical conclusion of boredom. All of us, it seems, are thrown on to life's conveyor belt only to be thrown off at the end and lost in oblivion. There is little we can do about it because, as Clamence said, 'We lose track of the light, Sir, we lose track of the light'.[41] Another alternative is to take refuge in idealistic views about man's achievements. This attitude is summed up in the oft-repeated phrase: 'I believe in the dignity of man and the glory of human destiny'. These are high-sounding phrases whose hollowness has been exposed more than once in the current century. Perhaps it would be more appropriate to ponder Francis Thompson's words:

All man's Babylons strive to impart
The grandeurs of his Babylonian heart.[42]

There is yet another alternative, religiosity. Its popularity is an
insufficient defence. It is no way forward to present Christianity
in narrow, simplistic, dogmatic terms which reject a reasoned
approach and rest in the false security of a bygone pietism.

If escapism and nihilism, idealism and religiosity are unacceptable, what remains? There remains divine grace. There
remains another dimension to the story of human life. The
ultimate answer is not with man but with God, or at least with
man's understanding of God's purposes. There are two impressive
conclusions which may be reached from a study of the Gospels:
first, that a way of salvation is proclaimed; and second, in
Dr Hort's words, 'He who on earth was called Jesus of Nazareth
is that Way'.[43] Mark's simple statement, 'Jesus came into Galilee
proclaiming the Gospel of God'[44] places Jesus in the prophetic
tradition. How did Jesus come to know the faith which he
proclaimed? He had attended the Rabbinic school and was
familiar with the meaning and interpretation of Scripture.
Doubtless he would learn about Moses and Elijah, First Isaiah
and Jonah. What was the significance of the lives of these men?
Why had they spoken to their people, what was the content of
their message and how did it affect their hearers? The first of
them laid down the terms of the Covenant relationship, the
second stressed the necessity of decision, the third sang of the
greatness of God, and the last emphasised the universality of
Israel's calling. All of them outlined God's action on behalf
of his people. So Jesus entered into a prophetic tradition which
already existed. Knowing the impact of the prophetic message,
Jesus adopted the same style when he 'came into Galilee proclaiming the Gospel of God'.

The things that he knew formally, he also learned informally
in the family at Nazareth. Belief in the prophets was fostered in
his home environment. Doubtless he was told by his devout
mother that some passages in the Old Testament referred to
him. Sometimes reference is made to the religious experience of
Jesus; what is meant by this? It means the truths that his mother

taught him after she had pondered these things in her heart. Jesus would also recall the words of John Baptist in the Jordan valley, 'Behold! the Lamb of God'. The voice from heaven confirmed the Baptist's words: 'Thou art my Son, my Beloved, on thee my favour rests',[45] and with these words the Spirit also descended upon him. The disciples corroborated his special calling: 'We know that you are the Holy One of God'.[46] It is important to emphasise this distinctive religious experience of Jesus. Not only did he enter into the prophetic tradition, he perpetuated it and himself became the focus of its teaching.

An authentic religious experience in one who was already in the prophetic tradition meant that he had something distinctive to offer. What was it? It may be summarised in these words, 'The time is up, the rule of God is here, change your mind, believe in the Gospel'. The Jews had learned that every activity under heaven has its time.[47] This was the time for salvation, something that is absent from the Preacher's list in Ecclesiastes. Yet they had expected it, looked forward to it, prayed for it, and at last it was not only possible, it was here. His presence was the rule of God in operation. They asked what it meant. He answered that they could understand what he meant only if they changed their minds. They had to change their minds about God's rule, about the meaning of sin, and about their attitude to their Lord and King. This is another way of saying that acceptance of his offer was conditional upon their repentance. We must now turn our attention to the all-important question: how did Jesus propose to change their minds?

There is, first, the offer of grace. God has graced our world with his presence. He did not wait till we were worthy or ready, he graced our world without calculating the possible results. He has come to us in spite of what we are. We cannot know everything about the mystery of God but we can praise him for what he has already made known. We may ask the question, 'Where is he?' then ponder St Bonaventura's words, 'His centre is everywhere but his circumference is nowhere'. Grace is God's love in action, showing us who he is, what he does and what he plans. We must always be careful lest the media of grace obscure the source of grace. It is God's gracious act to enter our world.

> *He sent no angel to our race,*
> *Of higher or of lower place,*
> *But wore the robe of human frame*
> *Himself, and to this lost world came.*[48]

We are graced even before we know it. We dare not contemplate how much preliminary work was done before there was a glimmer of response from us. God speaks and draws near and creates the conditions which make our response possible. He is the appetite as well as the food. He is the thirst in our souls but he is the fountain too. He runs to meet his wayward son even when his son is a great way off. Thus a deep truth is enshrined in the line:

> *He loved me e'er I knew him.*[49]

This is what is meant by saying that grace is free. It is free in the sense that we can do nothing to deserve it. It is free in the sense that it is unmerited, unrestricted and effectual. It includes all, for the way of salvation is a universal way. It breaks down all barriers of race, class, creed and culture. All God's work is a work of grace. We shall not see the end of the work of God because there is no end to his saving purposes.

There is also the offer of God's mercy. Mercy is that aspect of God's character which is shown to us. There may be other aspects which we can neither see nor understand but life is made up of receiving invisible blessings. Mercy is our greatest need. We can manage without many things but not without this. If there is one indispensable and comprehensive prayer it must be, 'Lord, have mercy'. The Psalmist (Psalm 136) was so uplifted by the truth that mercy does not fail that he mentions the fact twenty-six times in one Psalm. It is not enough to say that man needs God, he needs a merciful God. It is little use talking to man about an impersonal, remote and intractable God, for man needs to hear words of mercy emanating from a merciful Being. His great need is for a God who speaks, loves and forgives. Thomas Bilney's definition of the Gospel is entirely true, 'The Gospel is the mercy of God hourly showered upon us for Christ's sake'. But to make such a statement on his way to a martyr's death honours the Gospel it extols as well as the man who said it. However, the awareness of divine mercy is not a foregone conclusion. Man has to be awakened to its reality. Saul of Tarsus had lost his way, having become blind to the love of God. His conscience had become dulled and he needed an awakening. It was an awakening to divine mercy. He heard the words of the dying Stephen, 'Lay not this sin to their charge'.[50] He heard the words of Ananias, 'Brother Saul'.[51] For if Ananias, one of the targets of Saul's persecuting zeal, could call him 'brother', surely a merciful God would not disdain to call him 'son'. Between these two experiences came the question which haunted his mind, 'Why persecutest thou me?'[52] For any persecution of the followers of Christ involved the persecution of Christ himself. The plaintive note of the question was itself an offer of mercy.

At times there appears to be an eclipse of mercy. When this happens callousness, hardness of heart and brutality prevail. Now it is part of the Christian calling not only to receive mercy but to transmit mercy to others. Who was neighbour to him that fell among thieves? He that showed mercy on him. In this way all of us ought to participate in the service of reconciliation. Paul states this clearly in 2 Cor. 5, God has reconciled us to himself through Christ. He has enlisted us in the service of reconciliation, and has entrusted to us the message of reconciliation. These three aspects are inseparable and they involve the ministry of us all.

Grace, mercy and peace are the characteristics of salvation in Christ. It is not enough to say that the world needs salvation, we must participate in its benefits and demonstrate its meaning. St Paul calls all of us to be ambassadors and this involves diligence and responsibility. A true ambassador masters his brief, faithfully represents his principal, and conscientiously reports back. We must now consider some of those who first accepted this awesome responsibility.

Followers of the Way

The religion of the Judaeo-Christian tradition is concerned with events, encounters and explanations. The events are of immense significance: the Exodus, the giving of the Torah, the Covenant, the promise of the Messiah, the Exile of a People, the Birth, Death and Resurrection of Jesus, and the event of Pentecost. Within these events there are crucial encounters with individuals, for religion is essentially a matter of relationship. But even the offer of relationship is bedevilled with problems. Frequently there is rebellion and defiance on the human side. Yet these encounters between God and individuals often become vehicles of truth. Truths which eventually constitute the essence of religion do not fall like rose petals. They come to us through the struggles and tensions of men like Abraham, Moses, Elijah, Isaiah of Jerusalem, Jeremiah and Ezekiel. Within these conflicts are rebellions, refusals, misunderstandings and even rejections. Almost every contact between God and man involves encounter. It follows that explanations and interpretations are needed. Nothing is self-explanatory. Questions are asked, doubts are expressed, different views are given of the same events, so that every aspect of truth must be sifted, examined and interpreted. Fortunately there has been no shrinking from this exciting task. The fundamental aspects of its message are enshrined in history, scripture, credal statements and religious experience.

All that went before was directly or indirectly a preparation for the Incarnation. Jesus never assumed that his gigantic task could be tackled by him alone. The call of the Hebrews as a people was intended to clarify this truth from earliest times. It was to be a corporate enterprise: God, the nation, individual leaders, the Messiah, the disciples, and the Early Fathers had their distinctive part. The kingdom of God meant that God's rule was operative in this world. It was therefore imperative that Jesus should enlist the practical help of those who were willing to respond to his call. A Christian is not merely a disciple, one who learns the truths of the gospel, but an apostle whose duty it is to go anywhere to spread those truths.

At the beginning of his ministry Jesus called, chose and

appointed his disciples. They were the first of many and their work has not changed. They were to be called 'followers of the Way'. He chose them that they might be with him. Perhaps this is another way of saying that he chose them for his own sake. He gave them time to get to know him and he gave himself time to get to know them. It is surprising how much of his time was spent with the Twelve. Sometimes he would take the longer way to Galilee for the sole purpose of spending more time with his friends. The seven-mile journey across the Lake of Galilee to Gadara was turned into an opportunity to teach vital lessons — the banishing of fear, the necessity of faith and the duty of altruism.

His loneliness was mitigated by their presence. Their friendship gave him comfort in sorrow. On the other hand, there were secrets to be shared only with the Twelve. It meant something to him that they had continued with him in his tribulations. Whatever agony he felt at the Last Supper, he did not hesitate to think aloud in their presence. The disciples were present in the garden even though they did not fully understand. Perhaps there was a burden that even they could not share.

> *But all through my joy I knew, I only,*
> *How the hostel of my heart lay cold and bare,*
> *Silent of its music and how lonely.*

Yet he did not disdain to ask them the question: 'You will not go away, will you?'[53] expecting the answer 'No'. The wistfulness of this question underlines his need of their fellowship. But their need of him was greater than they knew. Sometimes it was necessary to curb their unwarranted optimism, and there were times when he had to banish their pessimism. However optimistic they were, Jesus never under-estimated his task. There was a constant danger that the disciples might think that things were going too well. Such an attitude might lead to an undesirable complacency. Yet the optimism of the Twelve was not unnatural. Their master had silenced the storm and done many wonderful works. Was anything beyond his power? The danger was euphoria. 'They are all looking for you', the disciples said. 'Let us move on',[54] he answered.

On the other hand, Jesus never over-estimated his task. On the contrary, he appeared to face every situation with serene authority and assurance. Sometimes his disciples reached the point of despair, 'Let us go (to Bethany) that we may die with him'.[55] But Jesus knew what the baptism of suffering involved and yearned that it might be accomplished soon.

In the midst of the hurly-burly of everyday and the mis-understandings even among his friends, Jesus might have been tempted to return to Galilee and live there quietly for the rest of his days:

> *And he loved Nazareth,*
> *And so, I think, on Golgotha,*
> *When Jesus' eyes were closed in death,*
> *He saw with love most passionate*
> *The village street at Nazareth.*[56]

But it was too late for that now. In any case, if he had retired to Galilee, it would have been an admission that the task was too big for him. It was not.

Not only did Jesus eschew that way out, he also prepared the Twelve for the tasks ahead.

> *Christ said not to his first conventicle*
> *Go forth and preach impostures to the world,*
> *But gave them truth to build on; and the sound*
> *Was mighty on their lips; nor needed they,*
> *Beside the Gospel, other spear or shield,*
> *To aid them in their warfare for the faith.*[57]

Jesus sowed seed-thoughts in their minds and gradually led them into the truth. When he knew that they had a measure of spiritual capacity, he began to unfold to them more mysterious and far-reaching truths.

There were certain experiences of the early Christians which were decisive in shaping the future of the church. The first of these experiences had quite a dramatic effect. The first disciples were Aramaic-speaking Semites, but within two generations the great majority of Christians were Greek-speaking townsfolk. This meant that Jewish influence on Christianity began to fade.

Greek was widely adopted as the written language and this brought astonishing success among the Gentiles as a whole. In addition to this, the Fall of Jerusalem in A.D. 70 compelled the Christians to re-think their position. The Jewish state was virtually annihilated by the Romans and the earliest community of followers was broken up. Many had to start life afresh in Greek-speaking cities. 'They were all scattered throughout the region of Judaea and Samaria, *except the apostles'.*[58]

Such events meant that Christians had to look to the future and adjust their plans. They also meant that a large responsibility for spreading the Faith was placed upon the laity. Although they realised that their history had prepared them for the present, their eyes were firmly set on the future. The phrases which came most readily to their lips: 'the new Jerusalem', 'the kingdom of God', 'the Parousia', 'into all the world', appertained to the future and to the fulfilment of their hopes. If they looked back, it was to the institution of the sacramental meal, the observance of which ensured the future of the Christian community.

They believed that their duty was to usher in a New Age, but it came in a different way from what they expected. The little company did not live to see their Lord visibly appear on the clouds of heaven. Instead of witnessing apocalyptic events which would usher in the New Age, they went one by one to their graves, leaving their successors to carry on the work. They were not dismayed, for death was seen as a necessary irrelevancy in the striking progress of the divine rule. In any case, they died in the sure and certain hope of resurrection to eternal life.

Their faith in their Lord was crystallised by events. They believed that he was as much the man for the future as for the present. His word, 'I am with you always, even to the end of the age',[59] was not vain hope but a certain truth which events would ratify. Jesus was no chance favourite of heaven, but one who had been destined to fulfil his high career in the fulness of time. He was a man chosen to shape the destiny of the world.

Doubtless the early apostles sometimes wondered what would happen after they had died. How could they be sure that the little community, in which they had played such an active part, would continue? In answering this question we should not overlook the impact of early oral tradition. This was one of the great stabilising influences in the early church. The magnetism of their Master was a subject for discussion and the outcome of it was a deep reverence for the example, words and institutions of Jesus. The commands to baptise all nations and to 'Do this in remembrance of me', were very precious to their ears. This was not just a sentimental attachment to moving words spoken on hallowed occasions, but the deeply felt belief that the continuation of the community depended upon obedience to his commands. The oriental memory is remarkable in its tenacity and there was much to remember. The sacred associations of those brief but crowded years became even more significant as his words were translated into symbolic actions in the sacraments. They were encouraged and supported by the fact that eye-witnesses who claimed to speak from personal knowledge of the words and deeds of Jesus were among them. Nothing else could have given such a rich dimension of authority and validity to oral tradition. Prophets and apostles arose in the new movement claiming to speak by the inspiration of Jesus and making him the centre of their message. The regular debates with Jews, with the disciples of John the Baptist, as well as with civil authorities, provided yet another opportunity for the daily proclamation of the teaching and acts of Jesus. This proclamation became an extension of oral tradition. There were also practical situations to which preachers had to apply the commands and example of Jesus, thus expounding his teaching. Should they pay taxes? Should they do good on the sabbath as distinct from doing nothing? How many times should they forgive an offender? The answer was to create a climate of opinion characterised by civil obedience, compassion and the spirit of forgiveness. The result was that the initial impact of oral tradition was extremely powerful and all this was confirmed later on by the written tradition.

Their main task was to communicate this message to the world at large. Their strong convictions about the course to be followed were quite astonishing. They were clear about the method of initiation. Converts were to be baptised into the threefold name. Passing through the waters of baptism, they emerged to a new life in Christ. The sevenfold gifts of the Holy Spirit were vouchsafed to them, and every time this ceremony took place, it was itself a proclamation of the Gospel and provided instruction in the Faith. They were clear also about the conditions of discipleship. The conditions seemed simple enough — repentance, faith, obedience and witness — but properly understood they have a far-reaching importance. Repentance is the first word in the message of John the Baptist, of Jesus himself, and of Peter's sermon at Pentecost. Turning from sin with all one's heart and mind is a preparation for the next step. Trust in Jesus as a person precedes belief in his teaching. Obedience is summed up in the command which is frequently made in the gospels, 'Follow me'. Witness follows from the other three since it is hard to recommend something which has not been experienced and tested.

The clarification of the aims of the Church is clearly stated in Acts chapter II: the prophecies have been fulfilled, the Day has dawned, the Spirit has been given, the rule of God is here and salvation is offered. In these words the whole gospel is implicitly contained. These remarkable events marked the beginning of a movement which was not limited by race or space or time. Truly it was a New Community. One of its most impressive achievements was to turn adversity to advantage. Even in spite of the fall of great centres of Christianity like Jerusalem, Rome and Constantinople, the Faith flourished, and these serious reversals served to re-emphasise the spiritual resilience and resurrection hopes of the new movement.

Even though this is a story of persistent expansion, there is little doubt that the trials and tribulations of the early days challenged even the staunchest heart. They were subjected to criticism, ridicule and persecution. Were they not upstarts, creatures of the day, ecstatically proclaiming a seven-day wonder? Indeed, compared with the triumphant history of Greece and Rome, it seemed so. Yet the answer of the Christians came swiftly. Their movement was older than the world for they had been chosen from the foundation of the world. In the words of Clement of Alexandria: 'If we do the will of God, we belong to the first church which existed before the sun and moon. The church exists not now for the first time, but has been from the beginning'.[60] The same theme is repeated in 'Shepherd of Hermas': 'The church was created before all things and for her sake the world was framed'.[61] Their forefathers, the Jews, had been divinely led, and were not the Christians also the children of Abraham?

Even so, a scapegoat was needed to account for all the troubles which had befallen the Roman Empire. 'Leave them to die', it was said, 'they are the maimed orphans of the world'. 'No', cried Cyprian, 'they have God as their Father, they shall have the church as their mother'.[62] Even natural disasters were attributed to the fact that the people of Rome had forsaken their Gods for the God of the Christians. 'When the Nile ceases to flood or the Tiber overflows its banks, the cry goes up:'The Christians to the lions'.[63] But the same Christians claimed that their faith retarded the judgment of the world and their presence saved the world from disintegration. They had, in fact, inherited a word of hope: 'He will not turn to destroy you, for he is God and not man'.[64]

If it came to the crunch, what could this weak minority do against Caesar's battalions? Again their answer was decisive: All things were subject to them and all things served their salvation. And what convincing argument could this small band bring against the eminent successors of Plato? It was a Greek philosopher who had himself become a Christian who supplied the answer: 'Jesus chose twelve men who went up and down and discoursed on his majesty'. They did indeed, and did so with striking effect. Their secret was the power of the divine Spirit and the only force that impelled them was the love of God. These were the 'followers of the Way' and present day disciples are nearest their true calling when they are near to them in spirit and action. For the 'followers of the Way' are also pioneers who began a movement whose ultimate result is beyond imagination. Well might they have said:

And yet the road is ours as never theirs,
For us the master joy, O pioneers,
We may not travel but we make the road.[65]

References

1. E. Gellner, *Crisis in the Humanities,* Pelican, p. 83
2. M. K. Gandhi, from an article in *Young India*
3. E. M. Forster, *Life of G. Lowes Dickinson,* p. 212
4. H. J. Blackham et al, *Objections to Humanism,* Pelican, pp. 17-18
5. E. Renan, *The Life of Jesus,* Watts, p. 227
6. St. Augustine, *Confessions,* Book I.4, Penguin, p. 23
7. John 16.22   (references are from the New English Bible)
8. John 10.18
9. John 19.11
10. Luke 2.29
11. John 11.25
12. John 16.28
13. John 14.6
14. Isaiah 45.21
15. Romans 8.16 and Galatians 4.6
16. Mark 6.3
17. Hebrews 2.17
18. Mark 13.32
19. Hebrews 4.15
20. John 4.7ff
21. Mark 8.29
22. Mark 10.2
23. Mark 12.34
24. John 15.12
25. John 4.29
26. John 19.5
27. Luke 23.47
28. John 3.3
29. John 5.19
30. Martin Buber, *Between man and man,* Fontana, p. 33
31. Methodist Hymn Book, 842.6
32. Matthew 4.11
33. Methodist Hymn Book, 47.5

34. Matthew 5.45
35. 2 Corinthians 5.20
36. 1 Corinthians 9.9
37. E. Przywara, S.J. (Ed.), *An Augustine Synthesis*, Sheed & War, p. 134
38. Methodist Hymn Book, 164.3
39. Genesis 4.8
40. Ecclesiastes 9. 14-15
41. Albert Camus, *The Fall*, Penguin, p. 106
42. Francis Thompson, *Collected Poems*
43. F. J. A. Hort, *The Way, the Truth, the Life*,Macmillan p. 20
44. Mark 1.14
45. John 1.34
46. John 6.69
47. Ecclesiastes 3. 1-8
48. Methodist Hymn Book, 62.2
49. Methodist Hymn Book, 423.1
50. Acts 7.60
51. Acts 9.17
52. Acts 9.4
53. John 6.67
54. Mark 1.34
55. John 11.16
56. F. Warburton Lewis, *Jesus of Galilee*, Nicholson & Watson, p. 15
57. Dante, (Trans: M. B. Anderson), *The Divine Comedy*, Oxford
58. Acts 8.1
59. Matthew 28.20
60. 2 Clement 14
61. Visions 2.4
62. H. M. Gwatkin, *Selections from Early Christian Writers*, Macmillan, p. 147
63. H. Chadwick, *The Early Church*, Pelican, p. 29
64. Hosea 2.9
65. V. H. Friedlander, from the poem: 'We shall not travel'.

The Hidden Way

The Hidden Way

The hidden way as understood in the foregoing pages presupposes a substratum of beliefs, ideas and values which has developed in different races and cultures over the centuries. This substratum has resulted from man's philosophical, social and religious explorations. It is an accumulation of truths which has been gathered, stored and tested in human experience. Its immense and varied richness has been recounted in the four sections of this book. Man is a pilgrim and an explorer who in some way has been able to cultivate and preserve those ideas, beliefs and values which he has found advantageous during his journey. Yet there is the tacit assumption that his development has always been inspired and supervised and sometimes overruled by a mind outside his own.

Man appears to be instinctively aware of the hidden way even though he has difficulty in understanding how it was formed and how best to relate it to his own experience. Perhaps one of the qualifications for receiving the benefits of the hidden way is to be ready to respond. It has been said that 'Religion is the total response of man to all his environment',[1] and our contention is that the hidden way as well as the controlling and supervising mind are part of 'all his environment'. It is therefore necessary for him to adopt an attitude of positive response. The opposite of this: attitudes of hostility, passive resignation, or a grim determination to endure, will not be of much help to him.

Here he comes face to face with a difficult problem: has any philosophical system or ethical society or religious doctrine ever expressed all the characteristics of the hidden way? Perhaps this analogy will be helpful. A train which runs on a track in mountainous country will sometimes be seen running across sunlit valleys but at other times it will move into a dark tunnel and will be invisible for a time. However, whether it is visible or invisible it is running on the same track. Similarly the light and truth of religion may appear intermittently and sporadically like the temporary appearance of the train in the sunlit valleys.

Maybe we should not expect to see all the rich and varied characteristics of the hidden way simultaneously. At the same time we can believe that each religion may offer a powerful and cogent expression of some aspects of the hidden way.

Each of the four religions mentioned tells us something about man's spiritual exploration. Taoism teaches us that he has to come to terms with the world of nature; Hinduism teaches us that he must come to terms with supernatural forces; Buddhism tells us that he must come to terms with himself, and Christianity affirms that he must come to terms with his fellow man although this may involve being reconciled to God. Perhaps the discoveries he makes in this exercise will lead us to the characteristics of the hidden way.

What is man really seeking? He is seeking a congenial environment. He feels that he must come to terms with the world of nature. Haldane's question to the inscrutable Sphinx — 'Is the universe friendly?' was worth asking even if he received no answer. Taoism had answered that question in the affirmative long ago. A sympathetic and understanding response to the natural world helps man to feel at home. And even though he sometimes feels alienated, it is only because he seems to know that he once belonged.

A tree is chosen as the Taoist symbol of the hidden way because any attempt to represent the Tao turns out to be the shape of a tree. Moreover, the 'uncarved block' is the Taoist way of referring to the beginning of the world. It may also be pointed out that pictures by Chinese artists almost always include a tree. Sung artists seemed to think that a peach tree must be included. A tree symbolises beginnings, growth, maturity, strength, beauty and usefulness. And ought not this to be the story of man's progressive development also? So the first symbol of the hidden way expresses balance and harmony in the world of nature.

Man has to do more than come to terms with the world of nature, he has to come to terms with supernatural forces also. In his spiritual development the time comes when fear turns to awe, awe to dependence, and dependence to worship. Within certain limits man was able to cope with the powers of nature, re-directing the rivers, irrigating the land, and learning to ride the storms. He learned also to deal with forest fires and to domesticate wild animals so that some of them became his faithful servants. There were, however, certain supernatural forces which were altogether too powerful, unpredictable and mysterious for him to overcome or even to understand. The Hindus devised their own way of accommodating such forces. They turned to philosophy rather than prophecy. They were less interested in foretelling than in forethought. They endeavoured to think their way through in the hope that they might create a realm in which supernatural, natural and human forces might fulfil their respective roles even though this involves interplay, overlap and a strong sense of direction.

The Hindus achieved this remarkable concept in three ways: by a recognition of the possible and the impossible, by putting supernatural forces into a form in which they could be handled, and by introducing a cosmic, monistic circle or mandala in which all forces and agencies could be contained and controlled. This achievement is to be viewed as part of the pilgrimage of man. It implies recognising that some questions are answerable and others are not, some problems can be solved and others must be indefinitely shelved. But by trial and error, by determination, skill and imagination, man was able to deal reasonably well with natural forces. What was to be his attitude to those supernatural, mysterious forces which he feared but could not understand? He brought them within his own orbit by naming them, respecting them and exchanging gifts. The sun became Surya, the wind Vayu, fire became Agni, and Mother Earth became Prithivi. Once these mysterious forces had been named, befriended and regarded as divine Beings, some sort of relationship became possible with them.

There followed from this the third and most significant development. From Vedic times till the appearance of Sankara in the eighth century A.D. there was a yearning among Hindu philosophers to include all forces — natural, supernatural and human — in the one circle or mandala. Sankara expressed what had been long believed, namely, the desire to unite everything in the concept of absolute monism. For such an idea the mandala is the only adequate symbol and at its centre is the only reality, Brahman. Therefore, if the first symbol of the hidden way represents balance and harmony in the natural world, the second is the comprehensive unity or wholeness which is expressed in the mandala. This archetypal mandala represents the whole universe and within it the cosmic connections of various divinities are often depicted. Insofar as human beings wish to see their lives 'in the round', that is in wholeness and fulfilment, it is entirely appropriate that Hinduism should reveal to us this symbol of the hidden way. If Taoism teaches us how to come to terms with the natural world, Hinduism shows us that the way to come to terms with supernatural powers is by including them within the universal mandala of our dreams and expectations.

It is doubtful if man will ever feel at home in his world until and unless he finds a way of coming to terms with himself. Buddhism may help us here. Unless the state of inward conflict is resolved, he will not know the serenity for which he yearns. The lotus flower has always been associated with this serenity. This symbol goes back to the time when the Buddha held aloft a golden lotus and allowed it to impart its own message. He spoke no word, the silent symbol itself being eloquent of his meaning. But this is not merely a passive silence, it has a content of its own. And just because silence brings its own rewards, we should be sensitive to the lessons of a 'filled' silence. In this way silence will serve our existence. For what we are is the result of what we have thought and not necessarily what we have said. We should learn lessons from the lotus. The flower rests undisturbed on the surface of the water as if the lessons of calmness and simplicity were more important than everything else. Its openness is a sign of unqualified trust. It patiently waits for the warmth that renews life.

> *For you the entire monopoly of the day,*
> *For you the glory of the immortal sun.*

The jewel at the heart of the lotus is the awareness of the still centre when all around is turbulence and strife. In meditation the open hands of the lotus position indicate surrender and trust. Silence, stillness, equanimity, openness and beauty are the qualities inspired by the lotus flower. Altogether they produce that deep serenity which withstands all noisy invasions and distractions from outside. Generally we experience only intermittent peace but this is something different. This is a constant serenity which is the result of acceptance and detachment. If we could find amid all the distracting and disconcerting experiences of our lives the quiet awareness of the lotus flower which makes no comment, presents no argument, but gently rests on the face of the waters, perhaps we could find the gem at the heart of it and the incomparable serenity which it evokes. Only so can we come to terms with the conflicts, contradictions and tensions within ourselves. Serenity, the third characteristic of the hidden way, is a treasured quality which is one answer to the pressing needs of a confused world.

One more thing remains to be done and perhaps this is the hardest task of all. Man has to find ways and means of coming to terms with his fellow men. Whether they are friends or enemies, careless or indifferent, he must find ways of living in peace with them. In our glimpses of the hidden way there is one problem which has not yet been faced. Is it possible for man to live peacefully and contentedly with his fellow men if he draws on human resources alone? The hidden way appears to be a pilgrim way which embodies the high ideals and noble expectations of man's life. Its qualities which have so far emerged — harmony, wholeness and serenity — are certainly to be sought after with sincerity and zeal. Even so, it may be that one more quality is needed if a life that is enriched by those virtues is ever to be attained. That quality is a disposition to accept, and then to offer, forgiveness. To find peace within, man must know how to receive forgiveness, and to live in peace with others, he must learn how to forgive.

Although chronologically the sign of the cross comes last in the story we have recounted, it may be that what is last in time should be first in terms of need. Perhaps this sign and all that it means should precede the others to give them credibility and meaning. For while it is entirely right that man should strive for the ideals of harmony, wholeness and serenity, the question is whether they can ever be attained without knowing and receiving resources which produce forgiveness and reconciliation. And those resources are scarcely to be found at the human level alone. While it is essential to appreciate the careful balance and intrinsic harmony of the natural world and to strive for that wholeness and unity which results from the conflux of the natural and supernatural, it is equally essential to strive for wholeness and serenity in the life of man. For he must learn to live in peace and fellowship with others lest mistrust, fear and violence wreck all his hopes. The vision of a new world may come through lives based on forgiveness and reconciliation and such blessings are offered through the Sacrifice of Christ. In the Cross we see the love of God and the sin of man, and through the grace of Christ the first becomes the answer to the second. In the end our salvation will be found in the answer which heaven has given to the problems of earth, and then giving back earth's answer in gratitude, loyalty and service. Then a dream will become reality.

> *And earth to heaven, and heaven to earth, will answer;*
> *At last the Saviour, Saviour of the world, is King.*[2]

We have postulated the existence of the hidden way with its continuity, variety and permanence. We also know that it has resulted from the storing of beliefs, ideas and values, which has taken place on man's journey. We have also reached the conclusion that harmony, wholeness, serenity and forgiveness have emerged as its principal characteristics. Unfortunately, we never see them all at once. We see rare glimpses at various times in history but we do not see the whole. We are limited not only by a gradual revelation but also by our imperfect comprehension of it. There must remain the hope that one day the pilgrim way and the providential way will converge. Pending that happy age we must accept with gratitude those aspects of the hidden way that are already revealed. But we must not imagine that because we have only glimpses of it on the stage of history, it is comprised of isolated units pursuing separate ends. Just as many races and languages are incorporated in a national culture, so also are many influences   and   ideas   incorporated   in   the   hidden   way.

"Into the bosom of the one great sea
Flow streams that come from hills on every side,
Their names are various as their springs,
And thus in every land do men bow down
To one great God, though known by many names".[3]

Supposing we regard each religion as a temporal manifestation of one dynamic reality, it will surely be inevitable that the same motifs, symbols and patterns of thought, will be made known at various stages of our historical development. Throughout the whole process we notice an overlap from one tradition to another, an interchange of ideas, and a strong tendency for one temporal manifestation to make up for the deficiencies of another. At the same time, the continuity of the same motifs will be a striking phenomenon. The victory over evil, the desire to establish harmony, the promotion of goodness and the unceasing quest for inward and outward peace, are instances of this. In the same way, the tree which is the symbol of Taoism and represents balance, harmony and renewal, will be seen to fulfil a similar function in other religions. Hinduism also appreciates the need for harmony in the natural world and achieves this by a careful fusion of natural and supernatural powers within the Monist mandala. The tree also appears as a prominent symbol in Buddhism. The Bo or Fig tree under which Gautama received his Enlightenment became the Bodhi tree or Tree of Enlightenment. A favourite koan is: 'Why did the Buddha come from the West?' and the answer is: 'The cypress tree standing in the garden'. The Buddha came to make people aware of the objects of beauty, growth, life and strength. Wherever these qualities are seen and appreciated, the Buddha is seen coming from the West. Moreover, Taoism and Buddhism are forever linked in the insights and methods of Zen.

We therefore conclude that this inter-connection and overlap is seen most clearly in the symbols of our selected Faiths. The Yin-Yang finds its meaning and symmetry in a cosmic circle. The Monistic mandala of Hinduism resembles the cosmic circle of Taoism. The Yin-Yang attempts to solve conflicts and bring balance to the world of nature. The Hindu mandala often presents the dancing Siva, victorious over evil. Such a victory is also demonstrated in the Cross, and it may be that harmony in the universe can be restored only when man has learned the lessons of forgiveness and reconciliation. St Paul's words endorse this idea: "For the created universe waits with eager expectation for God's sons to be revealed" (Rom 8.19) Moreover, in the vision of the Holy City the visionary saw on the banks of the river a tree of life, "And the leaves of the tree serve for the healing of the nations". (Rev. 22.3) The lotus flower is invariably presented within a mandala and a Cross is an implicit part of the pattern. This may mean that the Cross is an indispensable part of the cosmos itself. The following words were uttered by a devotee who sought the blessing won by Siva's victory:

> *Thou mad'st me thine,*
> *Didst fiery poison eat, pitying poor souls,*
> *That I might thine ambrosia taste,*
> *I, meanest one.*

So also when the Christian seeks the benefits of his Lord's Passion, he sings:

> *Inscribed upon the Cross we see*
> *In shining letters: God is love,*
> *He bears our sins upon the tree,*
> *He brings us mercy from above.*

So in the end it is clear that we need the harmony produced by the Tao, the wholeness as depicted by the mandala, the serenity of the Lotus, and the Cross which shows in shining letters: 'God is love'.

References

1. C. A. Coulson, *Science and Christian Belief*, Oxford, p. 105
2. Methodist Hymn Book, 809.4
3. South Indian Folk Song

Glossary

Ahimsá	Non-violence, denotes the refusal to injure any living thing and the resolve to promote positive qualities like goodness and truth. The word was given wide usage by Mahátma Gandhi in his campaign for Independence.
Arjuna	The name of a warrior who engaged in a rewarding dialogue with Krishna in the Bhagavad Gítá.
Átman	Individual soul or 'self'. In Hindu teaching the union of Atman with Brahman is the goal of human existence.
Bhagavad Gítá	Song of the Lord. A greatly valued devotional book in India, part of the Mahábhárata (Great Epic).
Brahman	Ultimate Reality, the One. Unique because untouched by the Law of Karma. The destination of all who travel the spiritual path.
Bráhmin	A person belonging to the Priestly caste. The other castes are: Rájanya (soldier), Vaisya (trader or businessman), and Súdra (worker on the land and servant generally).
Dharma	Pronounced 'Dhurr-ma'. The principle of cosmic, social and individual order. The word also denotes duty or calling.
Dravidian	A descendant of the Dravidian race. The Dravidians inhabited the ancient Shola kingdom of South India from earliest times.
Gitanjali	'Song Offerings'. The title of Tagore's excellent volume of prose-poetry.
Guru	A spiritual counsellor and guide.
Hatha (Yoga)	Pronounced 'Hatta'. A method of seeking union with Brahman through physical discipline and breath-control.

Harijan	'Hari' is another name for Lord Krishna. 'Jan' means child. Hence Harijans means 'Children of the Lord'.
Kailas	The Hindu heaven traditionally located in the Himalayas.
Karma	Pronounced 'Kurr-ma'. Action, work. The Law of Karma means that present actions determine the nature of an individual's next existence.
Kierkegaard, Søren	Danish theologian sometimes known as the father of religious Existentialism.
Li	Pronounced 'Lee'. A Chinese word signifying religious ceremonial, rules of conduct and social convention.
Macrocosm	Great world, universe.
Mandala	A circle symbolising wholeness and harmony. Some mandalas are works of art produced after times of meditation.
Microcosm	Man viewed as the epitome of the universe.
Moksha	Liberation, salvation.
Náráyana	Another name for Vishnu.
Nirvána	The goal to which the Buddhist aspires to find Enlightenment.
Puránas	Ancient stories about Hindu saints emphasising their devotion and altruism.
Rája (Yoga)	Seeking union with Brahman through knowledge, which generally involves a profound study of Vedanta philosophy.
Shari'a	The basis of secular and spiritual law in Islam.
Skandhas	A Buddhist concept indicating the five elements which constitute human life: body, perceptions, senses, will and consciousness.
Súfi	A nomadic saint and mystic in Islam.
Sung	A Chinese dynasty 960-1279. Renowned for its achievements in art and literature.
Tao	Pronounced 'Dow' as in 'plough'. Way or Path. It refers to a pervading principle in nature as well as a moral and spiritual Way for mankind.

T'ang	Chinese dynasty 618-906. Renowned for China's greatest poets — Lí Pó, Tú Fú, and Po Chü-i among others. Chü-i is pronounced 'Jooee'.
Tao Te Ching	Pronounced 'Dow Day Jing', the title of Lao Tsu's book *The Way and Its Power*.
T'ien	Chinese word for heaven.
Trimurti	Pronounced 'Trimoorti'. Three principal gods of Hinduism: Brahma, Vishnu and Siva (pronounced Sheeva). Brahma is not to be confused with Brahman, the concept of the Absolute which transcends all others.
Upanishads	Sacred writings of Hinduism containing philosophical speculations. This teaching was further developed by two great philosophers — Sankara (8th century) and Ramanuja (11th century).
Vedas	Ancient Hindu Scriptures. The Rigveda contains some of the finest prayers and praises from ancient times.
Yang-Yin	A Taoist principle which maintains that life's basic opposing forces — good and evil, light and darkness, strength and weakness — complement and counter-balance each other. This balance in any area proves to be beneficial to man.
Yoga	A salutary discipline of body, mind and spirit.
Yogin	A devotee, especially one who practises Yoga.